Coloring the Halls of Ivy

Coloring the Halls of Ivy

Leadership & Diversity in the Academy

JOSEPHINE D. DAVIS
Editor

Foreword by Reginald Wilson

Anker Publishing Company, Inc.
Bolton, MA

COLORING THE HALLS OF IVY
Leadership & Diversity in the Academy

Copyright © 1994 by Anker Publishing Company, Inc. All rights reserved. Printed in the United States of America. No part of this publication may be reproduced or distributed in any form or by any means, electronic or mechanical, including photocopying, recording, or by any information storage and retrieval system, without the prior written consent of the publisher.

ISBN 0–9627042–9–6

Composition by Deerfoot Studios.
Cover Design by Marianna Montuori.
Cover Illustration by Ernest Garthwaite.

Anker Publishing Company, Inc.
176 Ballville Road
P.O. Box 249
Bolton, MA 01740–0249

Contents

Acknowledgements	*vii*
Foreword	*xi*
1. Introduction JOSEPHINE D. DAVIS	1
2. The President's Role In Shaping the Culture of Academic Institutions F. C. RICHARDSON	13
3. Facilitating Change BARBARA N. ANDERSON & HARRIS T. TRAVIS	25
4. Reflections of a "Mother Confessor": African American Women's Roles and Power Relationships in Historically White Institutions HILDA RICHARDS	37
5. The Role of Female Chief Academic Officers in Institutionalizing Cultural Diversity in the Academy YOLANDA T. MOSES	45
6. Things They Don't Teach You About Being a Dean BERNARD OLIVER & JOSEPHINE D. DAVIS	59
7. Dispelling Myths, Affecting Change: A Dominican Woman's Journey Through the Groves of Academe DAISY COCCO DE FILIPPIS	71

8. *Recruitment and Retention of Minority Faculty and Students on Historically White Campuses*   87
DAVID W. WILLIAMS

9. *Recruitment, Retention and Graduation of African American and Other Minority Students*   101
DAVID W. WILLIAMS

10. *Queenie: A Case Study on Racial, Cultural and Gender Dimensions of Leadership*   113
JOSEPHINE D. DAVIS

11. *Eight Principles for Promoting Diversity with Dignity*   123
JOSEPHINE D. DAVIS

12. *Epilogue: A Visionary Leader in Challenging Times*   131
DEBRA H. LU & JUDITH KILBORN

Acknowledgements

At an annual meeting of the American Association for State Colleges and Universities (AASCU), a panel of women vice presidents of academic affairs convened to counsel Mary, one of our colleagues, through a campus crisis. Clearly, she was enmeshed in a "glass ceiling" triangle in which the college president had joined alliances with the academic deans to disavow recent personnel decisions Mary had rendered. This action surprised Mary who thought she had been hired to "clean house."

The vice presidents offered Mary advice tailored to each woman's personal experiences and unique campus situation. Interestingly, as the session ended, Mary responded emotionally to the experiences shared by her African American colleagues. "It's difficult enough being a white female administrator. I really don't think, after listening to your stories, that I could also withstand the pressures of being an African American administrator," she concluded.

Mary was right. Ours was a different experience. While credentials and administrative experiences may be comparable, the added dimension of skin color exacts of administrators of color skills, talents, patience, and prayers that nonminority administrators do not have to employ as frequently. Yet, such personal stories are rarely discussed within the institutions where they occur. Neither are they known by the public at large. I, therefore, owe a debt of gratitude to my AASCU colleagues for encouraging me to illuminate these subtle challenges by editing this volume.

Coloring the Halls of Ivy opens the dialogue on the experiences of administrators of color within the context of diversifying the leadership of the nation's public colleges and universities. Some of the narratives in the book may be difficult and painful to read. Many were equally as challenging to write. Nonetheless, each depicts the climate for diversity realistically in the hope that lessons will be learned. Perhaps, then, leaders of color will not be subjected to the same experiences many of us face today.

This volume is not intended to be representative of the experiences of all administrators of color in academe. There are many whose views are not presented in this volume. However, in looking collectively at the common experiences of the authors, one is able to construct a mosaic from which selected generalizations can be made. We believe these narratives must be told to empower the next generation of leaders to advance beyond the paralysis of today's paradigm.

I acknowledge with pride the contributors who assisted me in producing this work. Despite very busy schedules, they endeavored to meet every deadline. I also acknowledge the support of my executive assistants, Mrs. Michele Jenkins and Mrs. Jackie Ziegmeuller, who typed the final preparation of the manuscript and attended to the details of coordinating this wide-scale project, amidst other duties.

To my dear colleagues, George Ayres, who coordinated and assisted with the manuscript reviews; and Reginald Wilson, who provided commentaries and wrote the Foreword, I acknowledge their invaluable support with thanks.

I owe a debt of gratitude to my husband, Gordon Davis, and son, Rodney Davis. Not only did they provide moral support, but created the intellectual space for me to complete this project at home, after a full day's work, in the after hours. They gave up their personal time with me unselfishly so that another cause could be served.

I am especially grateful to artist Ernest Garthwaite for

capturing the book's message visually for those whose filters may be closed to other forms of communication on the topic of diversity.

As I travel this country conducting diversity workshops, increasingly more nonminorities admit their weariness with further discussions on diversity. But we must sustain the dialogue on diversity at every level of the academy until interculturalism is achieved. Its need is made manifest by the increased incidences of racial and ethnic intolerant acts on the nation's campuses.

Josephine D. Davis
Editor

Foreword

> The change in the composition of our society is not a one-time problem to be solved but part of a changed reality that we will spend the rest of our lives dealing with.
> *Dialogues for Diversity*
> Donald Gerth and Stephen Weiner, editors.

Indeed, ethnic diversity is a permanent fact of life in American society. However, despite its growing importance in the past two decades, we are still struggling to accept it as such. The struggle has been most conspicuous on the campuses of our institutions of higher learning. The surprising news is that people of color now constitute almost a quarter of the undergraduate student body and are its fastest growing component. The disturbing news is that as this proportion of students grows, the number of racial conflicts on campus grows as well. Students of color and majority students find themselves competing over scarce resources—enrollment restrictions with rising tuition—in a low-consensus society. This inevitably leads to conflict, requiring astute leadership from campus administrators.

Just as we celebrate the increased presence of people of color in the student body, we bemoan their scarcity in leadership positions at colleges and universities, as well as the heightened pressures and challenges they must contend with in these turbulent times. In addition to the usual issues—student conflicts, declining state budgets—minority administrators face constant questioning of their competence and ability to lead.

Minority presidents and chief academic officers must always be on guard against the tendency of governing boards to micro-manage their institutions, sometimes with the best of intentions, but often implying paternalism and doubts about their leadership ability. As James Fisher emphatically states in his book on presidential leadership, "If the board had properly delegated to the president the responsibility and authority for running the institution the president would be perceived to be the agent of the board with its complete mandate."

In addition, the minority administrator must be sure that his or her academic values are congruent with those of the board, particularly in sensitive areas in which racial concerns may be a factor in dealing with students and subordinates. Moreover, the minority administrator is often seen as owing a special responsibility to the larger minority community which must be addressed without neglecting campus duties.

Coloring the Halls of Ivy speaks eloquently to the concerns expressed here, as well as to many other leadership challenges that confront academic leaders of color. It consists of essays by administrators who have met these problems of predominantly white campuses and overcome them. Their observations are both philosophically astute and down-to-earth. As a former college president, I can attest to their accuracy and wish that I had the benefit of such wisdom at the beginning of my tenure. Aspiring minority academic leaders, as well as the larger collegiate community, will find this book very rich and insightful in the challenges facing the growing number of leaders of color in our colleges and universities.

Reginald Wilson
Senior Scholar
American Council on Education

1

Introduction

JOSEPHINE D. DAVIS

Josephine D. Davis is the third president of York College and the first African American woman appointed to the presidency of a senior college in the City University of New York (CUNY) System. She received her Ed.D. in Mathematics Education from Rutgers University and is the former Vice President for Academic Affairs at St. Cloud State University where she directed international programs of study. She has served as Dean of the Graduate School at Albany State College. Her research and writings focus on ways to improve education in the sciences and mathematics, the introduction of culturally relevant curricula, and the development of leadership skills among young people, minorities and women. She serves on a number of national committees, including the American Council on Education's Commission of Minorities in Higher Education and the Women's Caucus of the American Association for Higher Education.

DIVERSITY WITH DIGNITY

Within the higher education community, cries of "Equity and Excellence" have attracted the brightest and best minority talents to predominantly white campuses. Some of these minority faculty and administrators have been warmly welcomed and have enjoyed long and rewarding tenures on predominantly white campuses. Too many minority administrators and faculty, however, leave predominantly white campuses prematurely. Chagrined and embittered, they tell stories of guerrilla warfare in the academy, of acts of isolation and exclusion, and other extreme forms of insensitive and inhumane treatment. Because of the trauma resulting from the systematic application of intense harassment and encounters with sustained resistance, far too many of these talented minority faculty and administrators become disenchanted. Some return to historically black institutions (HBIs); others decide to leave the education profession altogether.

Based on the shared experiences of administrators of color from various ethnic backgrounds nationally, it appears that the true barometer of institutional commitment to diversity is not the number of minority students present on a campus in a given year. Rather, the litmus test of institutional commitment to diversity is the number of senior-level administrators of color remaining at the institution with a tenure of four or more years. Certainly, five years or more reflect an excellent benchmark for institutional commitment to diversity.

As the twenty-first century beckons, it appears that many of those who cried, "Equity and Excellence" were not sincere. Given the challenging and debilitating experiences of a large number of minorities who answered that call, the contributors to this publication propose that the clarion call for the nineties and beyond is, "Diversity with Dignity."

The achievement of ethnically diverse academic environments which work well for *all* students and administrators must be our goal. Likewise, emotional as well as physical safety must be guaranteed if, as a democratic nation, we are to achieve and maintain a diverse and enlightened citizenry.

EMPOWERING THE LEADERSHIP

Nearly ten years ago, the National Association for Equal Opportunity in Higher Education sponsored a national conference to address the concerns of African Americans on predominantly white campuses (PWCs). The proceedings of this conference were recorded in *Blacks on White Campuses* (Elam, 1983), which acknowledged that African Americans on PWCs, like their colleagues at historically black campuses, need to have "the opportunity to be centrally engaged in campus activities." The publication was well-received by the higher education community and its unique documentation of diversity efforts during the eighties is unparalleled. Furthermore, it opened the dialogue on the sensitive subject of racism in institutions of higher education.

Despite these ground-breaking achievements, *Blacks on White Campuses* focuses primarily on the conditions of minority students on PWCs, overlooking those of minority administrators. Today, it is generally recognized that full attention must be given to the condition of minority administrators on PWCs; for what is happening—or not happening—to them on these campuses directly affects the retention of minority students. Minority administrators play monumental roles in making "chilly" campus climates more welcoming to students of color. This fact, however, is hardly known and rarely celebrated.

Coloring the Halls of Ivy strives to change this awareness state. Reporting the experiences of senior- and mid-level minority administrators rather than students, *Coloring the Halls of Ivy* reveals the significant advancements that can be made with the active support of courageous, committed leaders. It is based on ethnographic studies conducted primarily by African American administrators, as well as those by white, Hispanic and Asian American women who are chief executive officers, chief academic administrators and other mid-level administrators in predominantly white, public institutions in Georgia, Minnesota, Indiana, Colorado, California, Pennsylvania and New York. Their essays chronicle the challenges, triumphs and crises they encounter as institutional leaders while highlighting their personal experiences as subjects, managers and agents of diversity initiatives. Owing to their administrative positions within the halls of ivy, these authors provide broad perspectives of the challenges public institutions of higher education face in facilitating ethnic diversity.

In the 1990s, more than ever before, chief executives and academic administrators who are marginally or noncommitted to diversity are often found at the helm of change-resistant colleges and universities. Their failure to support their minority members is a major factor in the derailment of well-qualified minority administrators. It has been determined that such high levels of benign neglect elevate stress factors in subtle, yet harmful ways. These leaders and their faculty must ultimately master the first step toward improvement which is to acknowledge their penchant for preserving the *status quo*. Once this hurdle is overcome, an architectural base can be established as a foundation for diversifying the academy. Ultimately, these leaders and their followers must come to understand the limitations of the environments they have created and are trying to preserve.

The underrepresentation of minority administrators in educational institutions is most commonly explained by the limited size of the talent pool. Other major factors, which are not well discussed in current literature but documented in this publication, relate to institutional culture—an aspect of higher education which is resistant to change. In addressing these factors, it is expected that *Coloring the Halls of Ivy* will open and expand the difficult dialogue on diversity. The experiences that administrators of color encounter in their attempts to fulfill responsibilities and execute initiatives as campus leaders need to be examined in policy-addressable terms. Such information could provide the framework for nurturing and developing an understanding of multiculturalism in majority professionals who suffer from paradigm paralysis—the inability to adjust successfully to different frames of reference. In this way, the educational community achieves forward momentum in pursuit of its goals for diversity.

Toward a Solution

Conceptually, coloring the halls of ivy is a complex phenomenon. First and foremost, it is a professional and a personal journey. It requires stamina and soul searching at a personal level. In the initial phase of this journey, some basic human values such as trust, respect, integrity and acceptance of America's founding principle of "justice for all" must be internalized.

In *Seven Habits of Highly Effective People* (1989), Stephen Covey raises this issue by asking, "Could there be something I need to see in a deeper, more fundamental way—some paradigm within myself that affects the way I see my time, my life, and my own nature?" (41). People are crying out for more substance, "…they want process. They want more than aspirin and band-aids. They want to solve the chronic underlying problems and focus on the principles that bring long-term results" (42). These demands, Covey concludes, require a new level of thinking. He proposes a "principal-centered, character-based, inside out" approach to achieving personal and interpersonal effectiveness (42).

In "The President's Role in Shaping the Culture of Academic Institutions," F. C. Richardson concurs with the need for a principal-centered approach. He suggests that senior executives need to shape their institutions around core values. He states that chief executive officers (CEOs) lead complex institutions in complex environments; and in their efforts to resolve the increase of unethical practices, he encourages CEOs to seek resolution by appealing to a shared system of beliefs. Based on twenty-five years of experience in higher education, he finds that life is "more civil and progress possible" in institutions with clearly stated and widely-known core values.

Coloring the halls of ivy requires community building; the forming of coalitions and collaborations between diverse individuals and groups. "Facilitating Change," by Barbara N. Anderson and Harris T. Travis, outlines a collaborative strategy for accomplishing change in a difficult environment. Using open communication and conflict resolving strategies, Anderson and Travis tell how they empowered others to transform the institution. Together, Anderson and Travis tell of the importance of focusing on the role of the university president as CEO. Although the president's actions are not elaborated upon in great detail, it is clear that the president of Southern College of Technology (GA) empowered his administrators to be independent decision-makers. The significance of a strongly committed CEO who communicates his or her values and states in unequivocal terms his or her position on diversity issues cannot be overstated. Strongly committed leadership is a common theme in institutional success stories. Likewise, where institutions fail to facilitate diversity, it is clear that the CEO either assumes an innocuous posture or takes no stand at all. Through this inaction, the campus learns that diversity is not a priority.

Coloring the halls of ivy is time consuming. It requires patience and wisdom. "Reflections of a Mother Confessor," by Hilda Richards, and "The Role of Female Chief Academic Officers in Institutionalizing Cultural Diversity in the Academy," by Yolanda T. Moses, describe the patience and wisdom required to endure the pains associated with the double-bind of being African American *and* female.

Richards defies the stereotypical role of "mother confessor," showing through deliberate actions as a "doer" that she is a person of substance. She comments on the fact that even five years into her position as provost and vice president of academic affairs, she still is not "as naive as to believe" that everyone has accepted her as an effective leader. Though diminishing in numbers, some constituents on her campus have a difficult time perceiving that she is a decision-maker, despite her gender.

Moses, as a "listener" and "facilitator," demonstrates persistence in her endeavors to alter culturally-shaped expectations at her institution which delegate that the chief academic officer perform only as a figurehead. Her presence at the campus complicates and further entangles issues of gender and ethnicity within an already strained governance relationship. The seemingly insurmountable barriers to diversity are easily dismantled when a new CEO arrives on campus. In a short span of time, the campus environments becomes less limiting as the new president clarifies lines of authority and communicates that his administrators are empowered to act independently. Again, the power of the CEO to alter change-resistant environments and to facilitate diversity is confirmed.

The stereotypical view that African American administrators are weak and inferior is not restricted to females alone. In "Things They Don't Teach You About Being a Dean," Bernard Oliver and I use a case study to illustrate the psychological battles administrators of color endure, particularly when making personnel decisions. The lengths to which some faculty go to avenge administrators who are perceived to "force diversity" are incomprehensible to the unsuspecting administrator of color who may believe that she or he can exercise comparable authority and power as do her or his majority colleagues.

The experience of a Dominican female who rose to academic leadership is remarkably similar to that of African

American women. For Daisy Cocco De Filippis, the challenges of the double-scourges of sex and ethnicity emerge again as inhibiting factors. In "Dispelling Myths, Affecting Change: A Dominican Woman's Journey Through the Groves of Academe," De Filippis examines myth-making and its consequences for people of color in higher education institutions. She identifies cultural and institutional barriers to performance and comments on her struggle between the expectations for Hispanic woman to maintain silence in public and her need to be more vocal over the inhumane treatment she and other persons of color were experiencing. Coming from a culture that values public opinion so highly that *honra*, i.e., honor, is recognized as a quality bestowed upon one by his or her peers, De Filippis indicates her difficulty with the initial hostility and negativity some of her colleagues expressed toward her leadership as faculty member, and later as academic administrator.

As her story suggests, above all, coloring the halls of ivy requires the courage to lead. In this regard, one of the greatest challenges for college and university presidents is to ensure that power is not consolidated so as to render ineffective the unempowered faculty and personnel. In "Recruitment and Retention of Minority Faculty and Students on Historically White Campuses," David W. Williams shares the success story of Metropolitan State College of Denver. He attributes his institution's success to its cultivation of a community of believers who value and welcome the differences people of color bring to the academy. Williams recommends the use of accountability measures as a means for keeping the issue of minority retention before the eyes of the academic community. He also challenges majority faculty to accept fully the responsibility to celebrate multiculturalism in all its forms.

Coloring the Halls of Ivy concludes with two essays which focus specifically on leadership excellence. The first is an analysis of a case study titled, "Queenie: A Case Study on Racial, Cultural and Gender Dimensions of Leadership." Individuals responsible for developing curricula for leadership development seminars, management workshops or other executive training programs need to prepare aspiring administrators for their roles as managers of institutional culture. This essay is provided as a resource for leadership development. The latter, "Eight Principles for Promoting Diversity with Dignity," provides recommendations for the reader and other influential members of the academy, the private sector, governing boards and various groups to use in enhancing their understanding of the experiences of people of color in the academy.

The epilogue, "A Visionary Leader in Challenging Times," by Debra H. Lu and Judith Kilborn, consists of information characterizing the influence of an African American female on a predominantly white campus. Having gathered their data from faculty and administrators, the authors provide a unique perspective on how the campus views challenges faced by a minority administrator. Also included is commentary on environmental racism and sexism, and recommendations for administrators wishing to hire and retain minority leaders on predominantly white campuses.

Coloring the Halls of Ivy aims to be instructive to the next cohort of minority administrators. It strives to prepare them for the lofty expectations that will be placed upon them as they climb the ranks of higher education administration. It also seeks to enhance the diversity initiatives currently under way on many campuses with the hopes of heightening public awareness of the inherent rewards and values of a diverse leadership team within a college or university.

Persons of color who read this book will find they are better equipped to respond to the subtle and invisible barriers within predominantly white institutions which may limit, if not completely stymie, leadership potential. This book is equally valuable to nonminority administrators and faculty who desire to promote and achieve a more pluralistic and humane community of scholars on their campuses.

It is to these ends that the contributors to *Coloring the Halls of Ivy* have offered their personal narratives of joy and sorrow, success and failure, frustration and reward. May their courage as pioneering agents of change in change-resistant environments inspire others to actively encourage and promote institutional diversity.

BIBLIOGRAPHY

Covey, S. R. (1989). *The Seven Habits of Effective People.* New York, NY: Simon & Schuster.

Elam, J. (1983). *Blacks on White Campuses.* Washington, DC: The National Association for Equal Opportunity in Higher Education.

Freire, P. (1989). *Pedagogy of the Oppressed.* New York, NY: Continuum Publishing Co.

2

The President's Role In Shaping the Culture of Academic Institutions

F. C. RICHARDSON

F. C. Richardson is the sixth president of the State University of New York College at Buffalo. He earned his Ph.D. in Botany from the University of California, Santa Barbara. He has served as Vice President for Academic Affairs at Jackson State University and at Moorhead State University. Dr. Richardson has also served as the Executive Editor of the Negro Educational Review and is a national consultant in education.

Since the early seventies, institutional culture and the role it plays in the decision-making process at academic institutions has been at the fore of social research. Most studies, in an effort to give form to this amorphous concept, first attempt to define "institutional culture."

According to G. D. Kuh and E. J. Whitt, authors of *The Invisible Tapestry: Culture in American Colleges and Universities* (1988), institutional culture is, "The collective, mutually shaping patterns of norms, values, practices, beliefs, and assumptions that guide the behavior of individuals and groups in an institute of higher education and provide a frame of reference within which to interpret the meaning of events and actions on and off campus." Taking a more generalized stance is psychologist E. H. Schein (1990) who defines institutional culture as "...what a group learns over a period of time as that group solves its problems in an external environment...." Drawing upon these two definitions, it can be surmised that institutional culture, while remaining open to interpretation, is essentially a behavioral, cognitive and emotional concept that provides guidance to those persons, such as college and university presidents, who are in decision-making positions. However, just as institutional culture guides and shapes a president's decision, so too does a president guide and shape the culture of an institution with his or her decision-making. Instances in which presidential decisions affect institutional culture include the manner in which he or she makes, or fails to make, decisions; the motif he or she constructs by honoring, or failing to honor, commitments; and the voice and audience he or she gives, or fails to give, to campus issues and initiatives. Oftentimes, however, presidents are unaware of their role in structuring, sustaining, or altering the culture of their institutions.

ASPECTS OF INSTITUTIONAL CULTURE

While the *raison d'etre* of an institution, the ability of an institution to pursue its mission, and the quality and effectiveness with which it achieves its mission all contribute to an institution's culture, there are essentially three basic aspects of institutional culture. These are artifacts, values and assumptions.

Artifacts are the symbols which hold the meaning of culture—language, rules and regulations, routine procedures, customs, ceremonies, myths, rituals, sagas, legends, stories and folktales (Schein, 1985; Kuh & Whitt, 1988). *Values* are the widely held beliefs about the relative importance of goals, activities and relationships. Collectively held values are often expressed as the "system of beliefs" of a culture. For example, beliefs about academic freedom and governance in academic environments are influenced by the values of justice, competence, loyalty and liberty. These values may appear as exhortations such as, "the institution stresses good teaching," "the institution supports research and scholarship," or "the institution does not condone intellectual dishonesty." Or values may be stated explicitly in college publications, like the following, "The college seeks to develop in its students academic integrity, intellectual honesty, and tolerance of differing views."

Assumptions are the underlying beliefs that undergird artifacts and values. In the collective, assumptions and beliefs determine the institution's perception of reality. They are generally learned responses to threats which challenge the institution's survival. While assumptions may vary by and within institutions, one can determine the operative assumptions by observing the institutional fit between current practices and espoused values. Institutional beliefs and actions should be congruent, particularly in times of crises.

THE EVOLUTION OF CULTURE

Of the several theories on the formation of institutional culture, the three that are most relevant to the issues of diversity are the Sociodynamic Theory, the Leadership Theory and the Learning Theory.

The *Sociodynamic Theory* of culture formation is based on a consensus-building model (Schein, 1985). Its attributes are: inclusion and identity, control, power and influence, and acceptance and intimacy. Defense mechanisms are developed to maintain shared understanding and guide solutions to problems. When these mechanisms are successful, a new cultural norm is created. When these defense mechanisms fail, organizations become dysfunctional. Typically, the Sociodynamic Theory addresses the formation of institutional culture related to such issues as differentiation, creativity versus stability, and survival versus growth.

The *Leadership Theory* of culture development is concerned with the individual's role in developing cultural patterns within an institution or organization (Hemphill, 1950; Stodgill and Coons, 1957; Fleishman, 1973; and Bass, 1981). Cultural patterns are embedded as a consequence of the values and assumptions espoused by the organization's founders or leaders, by entrepreneurs, or by company owners. The individual's role as a determinant of culture derives from such functions as initiating and testing for consensus, building and maintaining the group, developing decision structures, and defining roles within the group.

In the *Learning Theory* of culture development, culture derives from either positive problem-solving or anxiety-avoidance situations. Culture is a form of protection for the group. Members of the group are comfortable when they can rely upon familiar feelings and behaviors. In the absence of a leader, or if the leader is perceived as a weak figure, members freely attack in the face of a threat (Schein, 1985).

CHANGE IN CULTURE

Since the 1970s, the academy has experienced its most profound shifts in the interpretation of institutional values and assumptions. If not completely eliminated, most institutional values have been blurred by the changing views of roles, responsibility and authority. Having been employed in four different higher education systems, I have observed that a sense of community is strongest where institutional values are clearly stated, widely known and frequently reinforced. Life in these institutions is more civil and progress is possible. At the other end of the spectrum is life at colleges and universities that are developing their cultures. These institutions evolve through three cultural stages: revolutionary, evolutionary and maturational.

Revolutionary cultural environments typically result when the institution is no longer able to resolve conflict through orderly means. Threats to survival seem insurmountable. The president gets a vote of no confidence, deans get fired, department chairs change, and, in this upheaval, the community becomes dysfunctional. When the institution exhibits competence in response to change, *evolutionary* cultural patterns show proactive rather than reactive responses to environmental threats. The leader of the culture is dominant and is not challenged very often. As the institution builds on what "works best," stress is minimized and institutional culture is *maturational*, i.e., evolving through assimilation and the practicing of known solutions. Adaptations to environmental changes are relatively painless. Protective cultural behaviors may emerge in the face of threats; however, they typically lead to adjusted cultural norms as roles are redefined, and power and authority are redistributed.

These stages of cultural evolution do not necessarily evolve in sequence, one from the other. Any of several external factors may force a "mature" organization into an "evolutionary" stage.

THE CULTURAL BEARERS

Faculty are the cultural bearers within the academy. They tell stories and repeat incidents that keep and transmit institutional culture as a vibrant, dynamic and evolving pattern of interaction between individuals and groups. Subcultures also operate within the broader context of the institution. Kuh and Whitt (1988) suggest that the struggle for control over key elements in the environment, especially the decision-making apparatus, often generates conflict among the subcultures.

In collective bargaining environments there is a growing contention that the union contract governs all terms and conditions of employment. The authority of the president is often challenged by the union as it declares exclusive rights over personnel decisions. As the academy responds to concerns such as changing demographics, which involves an increased presence of minorities and women in decision-making positions, the processes for facilitating multiculturalism and for managing debates on access, speech codes, and equal rights are hotly contested.

Different power circles operating as subcultures with unique solutions to these issues are becoming increasingly adamant that theirs should be the institution's solution. How to achieve a balance among these subcultures is a major crisis facing presidents today. Bennis (1989), in *Why Leaders Can't Lead,* suggests that the resulting division and dissipation of power and authority has resulted in too many chiefs. Institutional leaders, hired as chief executive officers, find it impossible to manage or lead complex organizations in the face of such challenges. In proposing a solution to this dilemma, Schein (1990) identified the manipulation of culture as the primary way for institutional leaders to achieve positive outcomes. By the time many new presidents recognize this solution, their first presidency is over.

MANAGING CULTURE WITHIN THE INSTITUTION

Several means are available to college presidents to shape their institutional culture to positive ends. Hiring practices, curricular reform and crisis management are some examples.

Hiring Practices. This is one of the most effective ways to change the culture of an institution, particularly at the level of the middle manager or above. The ability, though, of the new hire to be an effective change-agent may be compromised by the person who orients him or her to the institution's expectations. Emphasis given to key institutional values and the transmission of institutional philosophy are important to facilitate successful integration into the administrative leadership team. The president must play a visible role in this area.

Curricular Reform. This is the most nonthreatening approach to affecting a change in culture within the academy.

The approach may yield no change at all if reform is not accepted by the faculty. Some positive outcomes of curricular reform for faculty are the reexamination of basic academic beliefs, renewal in the intent of the enterprise by the discovery of colleagues and scholars across disciplinary lines, and growth in enthusiasm for other projects. Faculty should be encouraged to take leadership roles in this area.

Crisis Management. In dysfunctional institutions where any form of change is resisted, the only way that a change in behavior, culture or direction will occur is through a crisis. It provides an opportunity for the leader to reiterate basic values and institutional principles which govern activities, behaviors and decisions. The crisis also affords the leader the opportunity to characterize the dysfunctional behavior and structures within the organization and to call for their elimination. Blue-ribbon panels may be created to make recommendations for change or consultants from the outside may be brought in to provide a fresh perspective.

Creating crisis is risky. Generally, there are enough crises existing within the institution already. The ability of the president to manage crises to the benefit of the institution is what Schein (1990) meant in stating that the role of leadership is to manipulate the culture to positive ends.

LEADERSHIP EXAMPLES

In my first three years as president of the State University College (SUNY) at Buffalo, I have had to manage several crises. One was externally generated; the other was generated internally.

Externally Generated Crisis

It was February of 1990 and two student leaders attacked the university's vice president for student affairs and the athletics director. The crisis developed when I approved a recommendation by the dean of students to suspend the student leaders. The crisis was heightened by the factor of race: it was coincidental that an African American college president was publicly opposing the behavior of an African American student government president at a predominantly white institution (PWI).

The two student leaders chose to seek remedy in the New York State Supreme Court rather than in the campus judicial system. Forty-one faculty members subsequently signed a petition asking me to overlook the incident even though the court had referred the matter back to the campus. Adhering to basic values and principles, I made it known that certain forms of behavior were not going to be tolerated at the college. The students were found guilty of violating the Code of Rights, Freedoms and Responsibilities of the college. A blue-ribbon group was formed to review the issues in the case and to make recommendations for future actions. From this problem situation, students learned that the "consultation" process does not grant veto power over institutional policies. Faculty learned that freedom with responsibility grants administrators the right to move about campus or remain in their offices without fear of being attacked by students.

Internally Generated Crisis

The internally generated crisis was the result of budgetary cuts. Prior to my arrival at SUNY College at Buffalo, the system's budget was reduced by forty-seven million dollars. This cut translated into a 2.5 million dollar reduction for the campus, requiring the deletion of fifty-six institutional lines. Three months were spent preparing a response as a worse case scenario. Fortunately, the legislature restored most of the funds. The initial scare, though, aroused some latent cultural defense mechanisms, prompting private meetings with the faculty union president, the chair of the college senate, the vice president and others.

By November 1991, when the announcement of the official budget reduction measures was made, a crisis erupted. The faculty union president requested a luncheon meeting with me to inform me of a similar crisis that occurred in 1983. She told me, "You can't lay-off even one employee. We'll attack as we did in 1983. You should know that the president eventually lost his job." In short, as a cultural bearer, she was delivering a warning, "Don't act!"

With firm but understanding leadership, I returned to the basic belief that the institution needed to make the best decisions even during fiscally bleak periods. Through a consensus-building process involving the vice presidents and faculty senate leaders, the budget was agreed upon, giving rise, for the first time, to a decision-making model for the campus to use as a means of addressing crises. The campus-wide response was positive.

Conclusion

Presidents play a vital role in shaping the culture of their institutions. In their complex and multifaceted roles, they shape the culture of the institution through decision-making, personnel practices, resource allocations and distribution practices, and their own personal leadership styles.

When hiring practices, curricular reform and crisis management are used to alter institutional culture, the leader has to be capable of demonstrating caring and nurturing skills in addition to traditional management skills. The institutional culture is sustained and shaped as the president demonstrates confidence in healing wounds in the face of difficult decisions, calms elevated stress and anxiety levels, and shows his or her ability to listen responsively to multiple voices. Such actions and behavior by presidents will positively reshape the culture of their own institutions and the academy over time.

Recommendations

- Early in their tenure, presidents should determine who the primary cultural bearers are and use them to interpret the distinct features of the institution's culture.

- Presidents should study the history and evolution of the development of culture on their campuses and become familiar with the events which etched prevailing perceptions and charted the values most resistant to change.

- Presidents must learn how to transform to positive ends the negative components of their institution's culture.

- Presidents should learn how to use campus crises to affect change that is positive.

- Presidents should identify and use nonthreatening means to reshape institutional culture so that proposed activities and programs, such as assessment, total quality initiative, faculty development, curricular changes, etc., are not resisted.

BIBLIOGRAPHY

Bass, B. M. (1981). *Stodgill's Handbook on Leadership (Revised Edition)*. New York, NY: Free Press.

Bennis, W. (1989). *Why Leaders Can't Lead: The Unconscious Conspiracy Continues*. San Francisco, CA: Jossey-Bass.

Fleishman, E. A. & Hunt J. G. (eds.). (1973). *Current Developments in the Study of Leadership*. Carbondale, IL: Southern Illinois University Press.

Hemphill, J. K. (1950). *Leader Behavior Description*. Columbus, OH: Ohio State University.

Kroeber, A. L. & Kluckhohn, C. (1952). *Culture: A Critical Review of Concepts and Definitions*. Cambridge, MA: Harvard University Press.

Kuh, G. D. & Whitt, E. J. (1988). *The Invisible Tapestry: Culture in American Colleges and Universities*. ASHE-ERIC Higher Education Report 1. Washington, DC: George Washington University.

Schein, E. H. (1990). Organization culture. *American Psychologist*, 45 (2), 109–119, 190.

Schein, E. H. (1985). *Organizational Culture and Leadership*. San Francisco, CA: Jossey-Bass.

Stodgill, R. M. & Coons, A. E. (eds.). (1957). *Leader Behavior: Its Description and Measurement*. Columbus, OH: Ohio State University.

3

Facilitating Change

BARBARA N. ANDERSON
HARRIS T. TRAVIS

Barbara N. Anderson is Director of Academic Services, Southern College of Technology. Ms. Anderson received her Master's in Counselor Education from Georgia State University. She served as president of the American College Personnel Association for 1994. She is an active member of many student-centered organizations and has presented numerous workshops on leadership development and diversity.

Harris T. Travis is Vice President for Academic Affairs, Southern College of Technology. Dr. Travis received his Ph.D. in Education from the University of Illinois. He also holds an M.S. in Industrial Engineering from Purdue University, where he served as Chair of the Mechanical Engineering Technology Department. Dr. Travis has won numerous awards for teaching and service.

The Southern College of Technology (SCT) had recently separated from Georgia Institute of Technology and become a free-standing college in the University System of Georgia. SCT was nurturing its new status as a separate institution. I was hired as Vice President of Academic Affairs and Dean of the Faculty at the college, becoming the first person to ever hold this position.

The college, at the time, had little diversity, and all minority groups, including women, were severely underrepresented in faculty and administration. In fact, there weren't any African American faculty. Further, there was only one African American administrator and one African American secretary. All other African Americans were custodians and laborers. The few women administrators were concentrated in the area of student services. Female faculty were limited to the Division of Arts and Sciences with one exception.

I remember my first day on campus. I had hardly slept the night before. I was anxious, wondering how I would be received, yet excited about my new career. I took great care in dressing that morning and felt confident in my new suit and tie and, of course, my highly polished, expensive black shoes. I felt a tremendous sense of pride that morning when I left the house, and thought I had come a long way since leaving the small town in the panhandle of Florida where I had grown up. I knew that if my mother were alive, she would have been very proud of her oldest son. And yet, as I approached the campus, I could not seem to fight off my feelings of apprehension.

My apprehensions were well-founded. I was the first African American Vice President of Academic Affairs in the University System of Georgia not employed at an historically black institution. My hiring was unprecedented in the predominantly white colleges in the system. Despite great confidence in my credentials, qualifications and past successes, I could not help but feel the weight of such an awesome responsibility.

That first morning the president had arranged a meeting to formally introduce me to the academic department chairpersons who were eager to "check me out." Unfortunately, the president was delayed, leaving me to go to the meeting unescorted. I entered the room with misgivings about being the only minority in the group and wondered, "Will I ever be able to accomplish the goals for which I was hired in an environment that presents so many challenges?"

I had been in charge of all-white groups before, but only after earning their respect and confidence during one-on-one meetings and interactions. Recognizing the potential for fear and mistrust among the persons in this group and feeling awkward myself, I knew that I would have to rely on instinct if I were to survive the first day, let alone the first year. I chose to play the roles of observer and listener in this first meeting—two roles I would play time and time again as I sought to earn respect and overcome suspicions and doubt.

No one could have prepared me, however, for the total lack of collaboration and trust demonstrated at that meeting. Every issue that was brought to discussion spawned self-contradictions and group disagreements. It was obvious that each individual had his or her own agenda regarding matters which might positively influence the campus community. I realized from this encounter that my major tasks would be healing wounds, generating a spirit of collegiality, and developing procedures to resolve conflict.

Developing a Collegial Spirit

Of all the challenges confronting me that first year, the most difficult was handling the issues pertaining to climate on the campus. Numerous factions had been created on campus as a result of the college's fight for independence. Even though the overall mood had turned optimistic with the hiring of a new president, many wounds needed to be healed. Without a mission statement, published statutes, or clearly delineated promotion or tenure guidelines, channels of communication were not clear.

The president and I began to provide structure and indicate directions for the institution without imposing our authority or vision on our colleagues. We were quite aware that faculty and administrative "buy-in" were essential for change to occur. Buying-in was a slow and painful process even though faculty and staff recognized the need for change and internal growth. Eventually, three camps emerged: those who opposed separation and had no intentions of furthering a concept against which they had fought bitterly; those who supported the separation or were new to the college and were ready for forceful and dynamic leadership; and those who saw both viewpoints, but were tired of the lingering conflict. Each of these groups was frustrated by the consensus-building model we implemented to promote change because its long-term benefits were not immediately obvious.

Although many methods were employed to build collegiality, the one which serendipitously gathered many supporters was my decision to delay refurbishing my office until each of the academic departments and many support offices were renovated. Also, by engaging in discussions with department chairpersons and being a willing listener to their words of advice, I gained support for the major changes I intended to make. I truly believe the little things I did were crucial in changing attitudes and gaining trust.

Change began to occur as multiple strategies were instituted to establish lines of communication. The president and I engaged the faculty in open discussion in quarterly forums called "chats." Consultants were hired to provide professional development in the areas of team-building and conflict-resolution. Faculty were required to attend a two-day planning session in the fall instead of returning to campus the day of registration. Robert's Rules of Order were used during faculty meetings to encourage discussions on institutional mission and governance. The systematic implementation of these and other strategies shaped the institution into a leader in the state and nation in engineering technology and related programs.

MANDATE FROM THE OFFICE OF CIVIL RIGHTS

In my second year at the college, the Office of Civil Rights (OCR) mandated the university system to increase enrollment of African American students and hiring of African American faculty and staff. Up to this point, I felt that race was not a major issue in my transitioning. However, I became apprehensive that the OCR mandate would tilt a delicate balance that I had, at long last, attained. Coming from a Midwestern institution where the African American student population was less than three percent, I was quite satisfied with the enrollment of eight percent African American student population at the college. Frankly, I was not concerned with meeting this OCR obligation. And, with the governance and structure-building challenges I was facing, I feared valuable ground would be lost if I made attempts to meet it. I knew the race issue would cause us to lose sight of goals we were beginning to accomplish. I could only imagine the setbacks I would face if the issue of race became volatile, causing the already simmering campus climate to explode.

Because I was the only African American Vice President of Academic Affairs on a predominantly white campus in the state, other colleges were looking to me to take a strong leadership role. African Americans on campus and other majority leaders interested in working in the area of diversity were looking to me for guidance. The pressure on me to act was intense. I knew I had to take a leadership position, but the next steps were not readily discernible.

Fortunately, a highly respected white female on campus, Barbara Anderson, whose belief system was similar to mine, emerged as a leader in this effort. Being very interested in multiculturalism, she saw the OCR mandate as an opportunity to make needed changes on campus for minority students. Known as a student advocate and respected for her participatory leadership style, she was not afraid to take the risks necessary to get others involved in creating change on campus.

The edict from OCR, which mandated the development of a comprehensive plan to recruit and retain minority students, provided a structure to involve others in the effort. It was critical, however, that this effort be articulated as a vision and not a command. In answer to the OCR edict to create a culturally diverse campus which enabled all students to meet their full potential, we developed the framework for the college's "Retention Plan."

The Retention Plan and Committee

The college's retention plan was written by Anderson. Included in this plan was the creation of a Campus Retention Committee in which individuals were brought together to oversee the development of the plan, prioritize its initiatives and provide evaluation. As chair, Anderson was given full authority to structure the committee and to suggest with whom it should be comprised. It was decided that individuals whose faculty and staff would be responsible for the plan's implementation would sit on the committee.

Even though the president and I gave the committee chair total support, her task was not easy. The absence of top-level female administrators on campus and the challenges associated with affirmative action made it difficult for the chair to assert her role as a leader. However, she made two decisions that led to the success of the project: to focus on programs that would be good for all students, and to unite the group as a team.

Strategies to promote team building were employed at the initial meeting of the committee. The chair opened the first meeting by reading the charge to the committee. She explained her style and stressed the importance of team work and a solid mission. She emphasized the significance of the role of the committee; everyone listened and seemed to agree. As she described the task for this first meeting, which was an exercise designed to have the group members share personal stories about their first year of college, the room fell silent. Not one person uttered a word. The nonverbal language sent chills down my spine and, although I could not tell by looking at Anderson, I am sure she felt the same.

The first step of the exercise required everyone to share personal stories about their first-year college experiences. The group became excited and animated, and I was surprised to see how quickly the walls and barriers began to crumble. I will always remember that afternoon with warm feelings and an enormous sense of relief. We listened intently to each others' stories, noting the shared feelings of insecurity, and compared experiences with mentors. At the end of the meeting, no one wanted to leave.

Once established, the committee conducted a needs assessment, allowing members to determine the necessity for programs and/or services, and to evaluate the success of existing programs. Also, the committee charted a course of action and prioritized activities on an annual basis. The committee met regularly and played a major role in changing the ethnic make-up of the campus as well as in establishing a more collegial spirit. In my experience with the academy, there has been no other effort towards diversity that has surpassed the powerful and positive impact of this one committee.

THE COLLEGE IN 1993

The college is now a leader in the state and nation in engineering technology and related programs. Enrollment has increased by over one-thousand students. Enrollment of African American students has more than doubled, and represents the largest increase of any population group. Instead of two, there are more than thirty African American administrators, faculty and staff.

An Office of Minority Affairs and many African American professional and social organizations have been established on campus. African American students are active as student government representatives, orientation leaders, resident assistants, tutors and officers in professional societies. In 1990, the college received the "Martin Luther King, Jr., 'Living the Dream Award'" for its achievements in cultural diversity.

Some other major changes accomplished include:

- Changing the name of the college and reorganizing it into three schools;
- Establishing a School of Architecture and an Advising and Retention Center;
- Instituting eight new undergraduate programs;
- Opening a graduate school with three graduate degree programs; and
- Requiring all new students to enroll in a First-Year Seminar Class.

Additionally, in 1990, the college was recognized by *U. S. News and World Report* as the "Number one, up-and-coming engineering specialty college."

Conclusion

Colleges and universities, like society, are responding to the call for change to a more diverse environment. Change in any organization is a slow process. People must be continually informed, communicated with, and educated on the need for, and benefits of, diversity. And as unrelenting technological advances, along with the experiences of culturally diverse students, continue to influence curricula nationwide, the culture of the institution will be challenged.

To the effort of embracing and facilitating change, we offer the following observations:

- Education is the cornerstone of an institution;
- Institutions must be diligent in educating all students, faculty and staff on cultural diversity and the differences which exist within cultures;
- Professional and staff development must occur simultaneously with mandated changes;
- Race and gender issues permeate all aspects of change; and
- Open communication and conflict resolution strategies must be employed and modeled by top-level administrators.

Recommendations

- Spend time assessing the situation before taking action.
- Learn through listening and observing.
- Seek advice from those involved.
- Be patient with people who are slow to change.
- Be willing to take risks and make mistakes.
- Enroll others in your dream.
- Always be an advocate for students.
- Recognize there is always conflict, so pick and choose your battles carefully.
- Look for opportunities and take advantage of them when they present themselves.
- Never lose sight of your vision.
- Whenever possible, accommodate those reporting to you before you tend to yourself.

- Never try to change matters that involve faculty without first understanding their concerns.
- Provide structure and direction without imposing authority or vision.
- Always maintain your sense of humor.

These conclusions and recommendations are simple. They require only common sense. Many complex issues, especially those involving people, can be solved simply with a caring attitude, a vision of what needs to be accomplished, a willingness to listen and an honest attempt at placing yourself in another's shoes.

The college has accomplished many great things in a few short years under the leadership of an African American who was fully supported by the college president. The commitment to facilitating diversity continues and has not waned over the years. There are many areas yet to be developed and problems of racial and gender issues still exist. But we will continue to pursue change until we see our visions and dreams become reality.

4

Reflections of a "Mother Confessor": African American Women's Roles and Power Relationships in Historically White Institutions

HILDA RICHARDS

Hilda Richards is Provost and Vice President for Academic Affairs, Indiana University of Pennsylvania. She earned her Ed.D. from Teachers College of Columbia University, and has been Dean of the College of Health and Human Services, Ohio University, and Associate Dean of Academic Affairs, Medgar Evers College. Highly recognized in her field, Dr. Richards is Editor of the Journal of National Black Nurses Association, and very active in the promotion of minorities and women in higher education.

Two years after assuming my first administrative position in a historically white institution (HWI), a search committee member visited my office. He announced his resignation as associate dean and voiced his concomitant interest in returning to the faculty. In our discussion he shared his misperception of me as an academic dean. He said:

> We didn't want a strong dean for the new college. As department chairs, we wanted the upperhand in running the college. In fact, we thought that everybody was going to be happy when you were hired....The provost had his affirmative action candidate...and we had a double guarantee for a weak dean. After all, you are black and female.

His confession that incompetence and weakness were the criteria used by some to select me as dean jarred my memory. As a child, when I was less than enthusiastic about my homework, my mother often reminded me that blacks had to be "five times as competent as whites to progress half as far." How incredible it was to come to understand the true significance of the lesson my mother had tried to teach me years earlier only after reaching adulthood!

More than a decade has passed since I had this awakening. Over half of that time has been as the chief academic officer (CAO) at a different historically white institution. While no one would admit that I was hired as a token or symbol, there have been enough situations to confirm the existence of a white male perspective that relates being "black and female" to being "inferior and weak."

Before entering higher education administration, I was a psychiatric nurse and group therapist working primarily with people in crisis situations. To my advantage, I have been able to use the skills and knowledge I acquired as a nurse and therapist for self-regeneration. Without these, I doubt I would have been able to rebound from the depression and personal crises engendered by the near daily barrage of racist and sexist attacks on my personhood. Additionally, I have oftentimes questioned my sanity for deserting the pandemonium of New York City for the tranquility and placidness of a university-centered, Midwestern town. Had I known the role I was to forge as an African American woman administrator at this new university, I may have thought twice on my decision, for no review of literature nor participation in managerial seminars could have prepared me for what I was to face.

ACADEMIC ADMINISTRATORS AND ROLE BEHAVIORS

Many studies focusing on attitudes toward women administrators support the position that women are often hired at these levels with misconceptions related to sex-role identification. The common tenet of these studies is that administrative tasks require masculine behaviors. Femininity, therefore, conflicts with the basic elements of chief executive positions. According to the longstanding myth, men are better suited for administrative tasks because they possess the desirable and necessary job characteristics: aggressiveness, independence, competitiveness, and the ability to make decisions and solve problems.

Women, on the other hand, are thought to be passive, noncompetitive, submissive and dependent (Andruskin & Howes, 1980). Women who display the stereotypical "male" characteristics are seen as "social deviants" and, as J. A. Ramaley (1978) states, should be avoided. Frequently, the successful woman administrator is not credited on her ability. Rather, her accomplishments are attributed to chance or to sexual connivance. Consequently, expectations regarding her job performance are lower than those of her male counterpart.

Dr. Rhetaugh Dumas (1979), studied the dilemma of African American women in leadership roles. In addition to sex-role bias, she found the existence of myths that severely limit women's power within organizations. Dumas states:

> Whether she likes it or not, the black woman has come to represent a kind of person, a style of life, a set of attitudes, and behaviors through which individuals and groups seek to fulfill their own socio-emotional needs in organizations. It is not surprising, therefore, that there is a great deal more interest in the *personal* qualities of black women administrators than in their skill and competence for formal leadership roles. (7)

Dumas found general resistance to black women performing in formal, high-status positions. She notes that preference is given instead to ascribing functions which reinforce the plantation view of the "black mammy." As such, the black administrator's power is as illusory as mammy's was. It is derived from her relationships in an informal administrative system. She must constantly put herself at the disposal of those around her. If this informal network is maintained, then her power is sustained.

Dumas also discovered that the demands made of black women in leadership positions far exceed the responsibilities of the formal position:

> ...the black woman in leadership is expected to comfort the weary and oppressed; intercede on behalf of those who feel abused; champion the cause for equality and justice...often as a lone crusader...[she must] compensate for deficits of other members of her group (speaking up for those who are unable or unwilling to speak for themselves)....Expected to be mother confessor, she counsels and advises her superiors and peers as well as her subordinates, often on matters unrelated to the tasks at hand. She is called upon to fill in for her boss in dealing with problems related to sex and race, to mediate in situations of conflict ...quiet the 'natives,' curb the aggression of black males, dampen the impact of other aggressive black women—and to maintain stability or restore order in the organization or one of its sectors. (8)

Given these expectations, it is no wonder that African American women administrators are a rare breed. However, those who are able to weather the trials use their strength to an advantage. They capitalize on others' perceptions of weakness to exercise their personal power. In cases where conflicts in role perception exist, two courses of action are possible. One can either change to fit the other's perception of her or his role or change the other's perception of her or his role. I chose the latter approach.

ON TO ACTION

One of the first tasks I undertook in my position as Provost and Vice President for Academic Affairs was to calm the fears of members of the community who were surprised by my appointment. I did this by assuming the role and behaviors of a *doer*.

I recruited an excellent administrative team, inspired stellar performance from administrators and faculty, and demonstrated astute fiscal management skills. As a leader, I embraced the feminine. Persons curious as to how I lived or what my home looked like were startled when I extended them open invitations to my home. Since, I have held many socials and celebrations in my home. Faculty, in particular, have commented on the positive feeling generated by these visits. Also, I have joined women's professional groups and have become active in a variety of community groups.

Slowly, the morass of both suppressed and overt anxieties and hostilities with which I was greeted abated. Moreover, when I was no longer asked the question, "Do you have the goal of making this a black college in the next five years?"(I informed the inquisitor that only thirty-five of the 600 tenure-track faculty at our institution were African American and that only 600 of the 14,000 students were African American), I knew the transition to full acceptance had come.

Handling white men's anxiety was yet another hurdle. I can recall a social event at which a white male faculty member approached me. Relaxed from one cocktail too many, he asked, "White men no longer have entry rights in the provost's office, huh?" He was obviously unaware of the efforts I had made to open my office to *all* faculty. I hold evening dinner meetings with faculty regularly. I write a biweekly column in the university newspaper and maintain high visibility on campus as well as sustain an open-door policy in my office. I make it a point to be available to all groups and individuals to discuss any ideas.

Conclusion

While I acknowledge there are limitations to my infiltration into the "Old Boys' Network," I have established power relationships with my peers—other vice presidents. They now recognize me as a person of substance—someone to be dealt with as a colleague. Through vigilance and perseverance, constant and consistent negotiations, I have established definite power relationships within the university, particularly regarding fiscal matters. With this success came respect and the knowledge that power comes from what is attributed to you, not necessarily from what you possess in some concrete way.

I conducted a survey focusing on peoples' perceptions and how these have changed during my administrative tenure. Considering all the responses, the consensus was, "Compared to a white male, you had more to prove; your trial was longer and more intense." I would not be so naive as to believe that everyone within the academy has accepted me. There are some who still say I am incompetent and that the truly competent person in academic affairs is my associate provost—a white male. However, it appears that those adhering to this stereotypical image are dwindling in number.

Overall, most "forget" my color and see me as a "leader for all"—an open, friendly person who shows compassion and is a tough decision-maker. It's ultimately the latter trait that people find more difficult to accept. Some still retain the view that a woman cannot exhibit both compassion and toughness.

I have come full circle. The therapist in me kept my strengths in focus, capitalized on my attributes, and utilized my uniqueness in the continued development of my administrative style. As long as I am African American and female, it appears that my mother's words will continue to ring true. I will continue having to be five times more competent than the average white male administrator to be perceived as having half his capability in acquiring and employing power in the academy.

BIBLIOGRAPHY

Andruskin, O. & Howes, N.J. (1980, Sept/Oct). Dispelling a myth: That stereotypic attitudes influence evaluations of women as administrators in higher education. *The Journal of Higher Education,* 51 (5), 476.

Dumas, R. (1979, April). Dilemmas of black females in leadership. *Journal of Personality and Social Systems,* 2 (1), 1–20.

Ramaley, J.A. (ed.). (1978). *Covert Discrimination and Women in the Sciences.* Boulder, CO: Westview Press.

5

The Role of Female Chief Academic Officers in Institutionalizing Cultural Diversity in the Academy

YOLANDA T. MOSES

Yolanda T. Moses is President, City College, The City University of New York. She is the former Vice President for Academic Affairs and Professor of Anthropology at California State University, Dominguez Hills. Dr. Moses has also served as Dean of the College of Arts at California State Polytechnic University, Pomona. Dr. Moses has focused her research and writing on cross-cultural analysis of social inequality, ethnic studies, women's studies and cultural diversity in higher education.

Nationally, associations of higher education have increased their interests in cultural diversity. Everybody talks about diversity, but few individuals know what true commitment to diversity requires. True commitment is not simply "adding students of color to the existing institutional structure and stirring." To be truly committed to diversity requires a rethinking of university structure as we know it.

Institutional change of this dimension is very slow and difficult. It requires strong leadership. As the keeper of academic integrity on the university campus, the vice president of academic affairs, who is the chief academic officer (CAO), plays a strategic role in facilitating diversity. When the CAO is female and also a person of color, this task takes on different dimensions than are traditional due to the ways in which gender and race issues moderate perceptions of power and authority.

This essay examines the experiences of an African American female who institutionalized cultural diversity at a public university. Her experiences make evident the subtle and not-so-subtle barriers women of color face as they facilitate change in the academy.

THE CALIFORNIA STATE UNIVERSITY SYSTEM AND ISSUES OF DIVERSITY

The 1960 Donahue Act established a three-tiered system of higher education in California. The state has 107 community colleges, twenty state university campuses and nine campuses within the University of California System. These systems are differentiated by mission. The primary mission of the California State University System (CSUS) is teaching. The University of California System's primary mission is research.

In 1988, the Master Plan for the state of California made explicit the state's commitment to recruit and educate the citizens of the state (CPEC, 1988). The early 1990s finds 388,000 students enrolled in the CSUS with 500,000 projected to be enrolled by the year 2000. Some campuses located near urban centers, such as California State University at Dominguez Hills, have no "majority" populations.

Throughout the 1980s, Dr. Ann Reynolds, former chancellor of CSUS, worked with the Council of Presidents to establish several system-wide initiatives to raise admission standards for high school students and to increase access for students and faculty of color to institutions within CSUS. Several commissioned reports and studies on diversity have been accepted by the Board of Trustees and distributed to CSUS campuses for implementation. Consequently, cultural diversity is a major initiative on the state's twenty campuses.

For the most part, these cultural diversity reports focused on issues including Hispanic and Asian-Pacific American underrepresentation, educational equity, student retention and advising, and campus climate conditions. Each of the twenty presidents, of whom there is one female of color, one white female and four males of color, was encouraged to implement the recommendations made in these reports. The irony of this situation is that the presidents being thrust into diversity do not reflect the diversity encouraged by the system.

On Becoming a Chief Academic Officer

As a native Californian, I was always interested in the CSUS because of its commitment to "educating the people of California." Since many high school students in the state do not have a college-going tradition in their families, the "business as usual" approach to minority recruitment was not working well in the CSUS. The challenge of successfully diversifying the CSUS student population attracted me to California State University, Dominguez Hills, in the Fall of 1988.

In 1976, when I accepted the position of Professor and Coordinator of Anthropology at California State Polytechnic at Pomona, I had no intention of becoming an administrator. However, I did embrace the opportunity to chair the Ethnic Studies Department a short while after becoming a faculty member at the institution despite my peers' warning that ethnic studies was a second-rate discipline. Throughout my two-year appointment as chair, I continued to teach in my resident department. Needless to say, this double assignment was taxing.

While my colleagues and I stabilized the ethnic studies department, revamped the curriculum and made it a viable and productive topic of study, my skills as an effective administrator were being observed by others. Shortly thereafter, I made a permanent switch from anthropology to ethnic studies. This move left some of my colleagues in the anthropology department reeling; after all, I was *their* only minority faculty member.

Two years later, the position of Dean of the College

became available and I was chosen as acting dean. Following a national search, I was chosen for the permanent position and went on to serve five years as Dean of the College. Regardless of the development of innovative programs which gave the college regional and national prominence during my tenure, I was receiving negative feedback from some majority faculty who felt I was not qualified for the position of dean. Frequently, comments such as "She's not seasoned," "She's too young," and "She's just an affirmative action hire," made their way to my ears.

In 1988, I accepted the position as Vice President of Academic Affairs at California State University, Dominguez Hills, where the student of color population was greater than that at California State Polytechnic at Pomona. California State Polytechnic was recognized for its mission statement which made it clear that a multicultural student body was valued. The response my colleagues made in learning that I had accepted this position was, "Why do you want to go there? You're black, you're good, and you're female, you could go anywhere!" The "anywhere" to which my colleagues referred is another manner of saying "prestigious white institution." Even during my interview at Dominguez Hills, I was asked, "With your record, why would you want to come here?" Both responses are typical and representative of underlying, yet unexpressed attitudes.

My adjustment to the institution was extremely difficult because of some initial, erroneous assumptions—the first of which was my own. It was my understanding that the institution was fully committed to diversity and that my primary task was to provide academic leadership for the campus. What I found was a culturally diverse student body: sixty percent of the student body was female, forty percent was white, thirty percent was black, fifteen percent was Latino and fifteen percent was Asian-Pacific American.

The faculty, on the other hand, was eighty-five percent white and seventy-two percent male.

Though the academic curriculum had cultural pluralism requirements, no systematic review of courses for multicultural or cross-cultural content had been conducted since the early 1980s. I soon discovered that plans to institutionalize diversity had been placed on the back burner in order that all could focus on the turnover in key administrative positions, including that of the presidency.

As the new CAO, I wanted to accomplish three goals at Dominguez Hills: 1) hire more faculty of color and women to balance the racial and gender distribution; 2) develop a retention model, placing faculty and student relationships at the center of campus life; and 3) transform the curriculum to reflect the more inclusive "new scholarship." I felt empowered to carry out these goals because the president who hired me embraced the same goals. I had no idea of the barriers that would surface to impede not only my personal progress, but the institution's as well.

BARRIERS TO INSTITUTIONALIZING DIVERSITY

The four major barriers that slowed progress toward the goals outlined above were: 1) a campus culture which resisted diversity; 2) faculty resistance to student retention as an academic issue; 3) faculty fear of change and its effects on their seniority ranking; and 4) stereotypic perceptions of my leadership ability.

Campus Culture and Diversity

Dominguez Hills' campus culture evolved from the 1960s when faculty and administrative decisions were achieved using a nonhierarchical decision-making structure. This model did not require a strong vice president of academic affairs. Therefore, the campus had never experienced a strong CAO. In addition, faculty leaders were accustomed to dealing directly with the president. As a result of this, there were several occasions on which faculty refused to take my authority seriously. After the president announced his retirement, I engaged in a heated debate with the search committee that was assembled to select a new dean. I was insistent that affirmative action be taken into consideration throughout the search. To this, the chair of the search committee said, "But you are just the vice president. The *real* president won't be here for a year. We'll wait to see what *he* has to say about affirmative action. We don't want to have to hire an unqualified affirmative action candidate."

Faculty Resistance to Retention

Dominguez Hills has a national reputation for successfully recruiting and graduating minority students (Richardson, 1991). Historically, most of the effort for outreach and retention has been in the Office of Student Affairs. Consistent with the nonhierarchical view of decision-making, some senior faculty and academic senate leaders did not think there was a role for faculty in retention issues beyond advising. They believed that students should be given the freedom to make their own mistakes. Efforts to strengthen the faculty's relationship with students met with resistance and accusations that the administration was being "too intrusive" on students' lives.

Faculty Resistance to Curriculum Change

Some of the departments and programs had become insular at Dominguez Hills because no new faculty had been hired over a ten-year period. With an enrollment growth in 1989–90, new faculty were hired. Of the thirty tenure-track positions filled, forty percent of the new hires were female and thirty-eight were underrepresented minorities. In 1990–91, of thirty new tenure-track positions, fifty-one percent were female hires and forty-one percent were underrepresented minorities. To orient new faculty to the campus, faculty development programs were established. However, some senior faculty felt ignored because they were not included in these activities to the extent that they should have been.

In discussions concerning curriculum development and transformation issues, faculty expressed repeatedly that they were being asked to do something that they did not know how to do. Budget limitations had made it difficult, if not impossible, to support faculty in participating in and/or attending seminars and workshops within their disciplines thus limiting their knowledge of changing trends considerably. Moreover, many faculty felt this was an additional duty. Likewise, the request to participate in retention initiatives, curriculum revisions were viewed as another initiative they were being asked to take on blindly (i.e., without sufficient knowledge or experience). Senior faculty demanded released time and reassigned time to participate.

Stereotypic Views of My Leadership

Having faculty and administrators second-guess my decisions is something I have accepted as normal. As leaders, African American females across the nation face the issue of credibility (Moses, 1989). According to Reginald Wilson (1989), Senior Fellow at the American Council on Education, women of color are placed in double jeopardy because of their gender and race. In my experience, manifestations of these stereotypic perceptions are illustrated in attitudes that compel faculty to check with the president to verify his support of decisions I make, or to constantly question and/or challenge my decisions.

Because I pushed hard for cultural diversity as the new president's agenda item, some faculty said that I was a "single-issue" person. In fact, during my three-year evaluation in 1991, a small, but vocal group of faculty characterized me as being "only focused on women and minority issues" and in dislike of "white males."

INSTITUTIONALIZING DIVERSITY

Campus Cultural Change

The president was moving the institution into a more traditional hierarchical structure for decision-making in which decisions and responsibilities move from the bottom-up, rather than from the top-down. He made it clear to the university community that the three vice presidents are delegated authority and are empowered to make independent decisions without clearing with him. Also, regional accreditation recommendations urged us to "get rid of cumbersome committee structures." There were over 200 committees on campus at the time of our 1989 accreditation review.

With the president's support, the responsibility for institutionalizing diversity was spread out to encompass all factions of the university, and some measure of success was realized. Administrative procedures and practices were established, and the campus developed a five-year strategic plan detailing how goals were to be achieved.

Retention as an Academic Matter

With the reorganization of the Office of Academic Affairs, the position of Dean of Undergraduate Studies was created. The primary task for this dean is to oversee all retention functions on campus and to coordinate the development of a comprehensive campus retention plan. Retention activities of the offices of student affairs and academic affairs are being better coordinated through this position. This dean also chairs a university-wide Retention Council composed of every person who has responsibility for retention functions on campus. In 1991–92, the major goal accomplished was the strengthening of advisement and retention functions. Each academic school submitted a school-based retention and advisement plan. Faculty accepted this approach to retention because it was viewed as part of their regular departmental and advising duties rather than as an "add on" or "extra work."

Faculty Hires and Curriculum Changes

The faculty development coordinator makes it a point to include senior faculty in any workshops or activities structured for junior faculty. Faculty have access to $50,000 for curriculum changes designated by the president. Distinguished from "research and scholarly activities," these funds are controlled by the faculty and are distributed to faculty who are interested in updating their knowledge and skills in curriculum development.

A mentorship program, pairing new faculty with senior faculty, functions to introduce women and faculty of color to the institutional culture. I also keep enthusiastic faculty apprised of conferences and workshops so that they can attend and, in turn, share their knowledge and experience with other faculty by conducting workshops and seminars on campus. By focusing on what the faculty do best—teaching and research—professional pride has been reinforced as diversity has been implemented in the curriculum.

Conclusion

My experience, from graduate school through the academic affairs vice presidency, has been a legacy of having to demonstrate my credentials. It is a given that I have to work harder and produce more than my white male counterparts to be taken seriously. I often say to audiences that true equality will be reached in this country when mediocre men and women of color and white women are hired at the same rates as mediocre white males.

The double burden of race and gender continues to adversely affect the upward mobility of women of color, despite their qualifications and experiences. As a CAO, I have had the opportunity to seek out, identify, and work with those faculty and administrators who are committed to change. Together, we have formulated a common vision to make our university a model institution for cultural diversity and educational excellence.

I achieved the goal of institutionalizing diversity with the support of the president, concerned faculty, staff and students. However, were it not for personal fortitude, unwavering convictions and a deep commitment to these convictions, my efforts would have been compromised.

The Dominguez Hills story demonstrates the power of committed leadership. It affirms Reginald Wilson's assessment that, "The academy has the opportunity to lead the way by showing the rest of the nation how to eliminate these twin scourges (racism and sexism) and become the better for it" (Wilson, 1989).

Recommendations

It is necessary for administrators of color to develop strong survival skills to be successful in their leadership position. They must believe in themselves and the job they are doing, even if they stand alone. They must understand that in some instances they will need to work harder than their colleagues and peers because they are the "test cases." Furthermore, they represent their cultural or ethnic groups. They must often establish support systems and mentors outside the college or university where they work and they *must* develop a sense of humor.

Regardless of personal strength, minority administrators cannot succeed on their own. Fellow administrators must help their minority colleagues forcefully and consistently. In view of these concerns and observations, the following recommendations are made:

- The president and other campus leaders must regularly affirm and reaffirm the institution's commitment to diversity.

- Campus documents, from the strategic planning and mission statements , to the criteria for evaluating what constitutes an excellent academic program, must state the institution's commitment to representing minority and ethnic groups. These documents should cite specific examples of how diversity can be achieved within the local campus culture.

- Campus leaders must include minority-group administrators early-on when groups are established to draft or review policies and procedures concerning sexual and racial harassment or discrimination. This is important because they, more than likely, will have had actual experience with the discrimination or harassment being discussed or will know others who have had these experiences.

- Leaders must see to it that senior white administrators are included in educational programs, workshops and retreats devoted to the discussion of cultural diversity.

Involving only minority administrators in discussions regarding minority problems contradicts the goals of diversification. By broadening inclusion, the campus will realize that not only is change promoted, but it includes everyone from the top down.

- The president and other top administrators should create support structures—such as mentoring programs, professional growth and development opportunities, and outreach to minority communities surrounding the campus—for administrators of color, just as they do for minority faculty and students.

- Presidents, when attempting to improve the climate for female administrators, should recognize the special concerns of women of color. White administrators on predominantly white college and university campuses often overlook the impact that double discrimination—racism and sexism—can have on the effectiveness of these women.

Administrators from different racial and ethnic groups are a valuable resource in predominantly white colleges and universities. They often bring new ideas, insights and frameworks to education and to solving administrative problems. However, they often are frustrated because their subordinates, their peers and their presidents do not listen to what they have to say. We know that students often drop out of school if they feel excluded or undervalued. Can we afford to have this happen to the small numbers of minority administrators as well?

BIBLIOGRAPHY

California Postsecondary Education Commission (CPEC). (1988). *Master Plan Revisited.* Sacramento, CA: CPEC.

Moses, Y. T. (1989). *Black Women in Academe: Issues and Strategies.* Washington, DC: Association of American Colleges.

Richardson, R. C., Jr. (1991, April). Targeting Minorities for College. *Washington Post.*

Wilson, R. (1989). Women of color in academic administration. *Sex Roles,* 21 (112), 85–97.

6

Things They Don't Teach You About Being a Dean

Bernard Oliver
Josephine D. Davis

Bernard Oliver is Dean, College of Education, and Professor of Education at Washington State University. He earned his Ed.D. in Teacher Education and Curriculum Development from Stanford University, and has been Dean of the College of Education, St. Cloud State University. Dr. Oliver has numerous publications in the areas of teaching and education.

Josephine D. Davis is the third president of York College and the first African American woman appointed to the presidency of a senior college in the City University of New York (CUNY) System. She received her Ed.D. in Mathematics Education from Rutgers University and is the former Vice President for Academic Affairs at St. Cloud State University where she directed international programs of study. She has served as Dean of the Graduate School at Albany State College. Her research and writings focus on ways to improve education in the sciences and mathematics, the introduction of culturally relevant curricula, and the development of leadership skills among young people, minorities and women. She serves on a number of national committees, including the American Council on Education's Commission of Minorities in Higher Education and the Women's Caucus of the American Association for Higher Education.

Since the passage of the Civil Rights Act of 1964, predominantly white institutions (PWIs) of higher education have been challenged to improve the recruitment and retention of minority students, faculty and administrators, as well as to alter their curriculum to reflect diverse points of view. Despite moderate and intermittent success, few institutions have found solutions to the major crisis of facilitating diversity on campus. Administrators appear ill-prepared to address the increased racism and ethnoviolence occurring on college campuses across America (Kropp, 1992; Blanchard, 1992).

Under the aegis of academic freedom and first amendment rights, more faculty, administrators, staff and students are able to engage in discriminatory and racist behaviors. At the personal level, these acts can include slurs, harassment and explosive confrontations; at the group or institutional level, such acts may come in the form of impenetrable barriers to recruit or hire minority faculty, staff and administrators (Viadero, 1989). In the face of declining numbers of African American doctoral recipients and teaching professionals, the higher education community must respond, for this loss of human resource potential imperils America's ability to prepare large groups of citizens for future needs.

Although the educational reform movement has identified the need to diversify the curriculum, student body, faculty and staff on college campuses, it has been slow to address the need to diversify the leadership hierarchy in higher education. The plight of African American administrators in higher education was evidenced during an informal meeting of a group of college deans of color. The group listed only twelve colleagues employed as deans at PWIs and noted the following: 1) the retention of African American administrators in PWIs is short-lived owing to the personal harassment and indignity people of color experience in the discharge of normal duties; and 2) there are "things they don't teach you about being an African American dean in predominantly white institutions, management or leadership development schools."

No leadership development seminar, workshop on administration, nor management school prepares deans of color for demands such as:

- dealing with psychological warfare and feelings of alienation;

- dispelling myths among faculty of the leader's incompetence and inferiority; and

- assisting majority faculty in overcoming basic fears of professional interactions with people of color, particularly African Americans.

Of all aspects of working in the academy, personnel relations is the one area in which racial tensions are most intense. The hiring, promoting, retaining and granting of academic merit to people of color bring underlying anxieties and fears to the surface. These psychological tensions are encapsulated as structural and cultural barriers which derail efforts to diversify the academy.

To illustrate this phenomenon, we present the following case study involving a dean of color's experience with hiring minority faculty on a predominantly white institution. The case study collectively portrays the extraordinary conditions some African American deans experience in PWIs as they seek to diversify the academy. It is not positioned as being representative of every African American dean's experience. Admittedly, changes in the environmental context of an institution could easily moderate these experiences for a given individual.

THE CASE STUDY

Joseph Cantor was welcomed enthusiastically to Harker University (HU) as the first African American administrator hired in its more than 100-year history. In fact, within the entire state university system which consisted of eight member campuses, Cantor's appointment made him the only academic dean of color.

An experienced administrator, Cantor had worked in a collective bargaining environment on a predominantly white campus prior to coming to HU. He was not, however, experienced with the industrial and noncollegial model presented to him at HU. The confluence of the institution's monolithic culture, its distributive model of collective bargaining, and its pioneering experience with racial integration exacted different strategies for management and leadership than Cantor was accustomed. His first challenge was to develop coping skills to fit this new environmental context.

Institutional Commitment

Cantor was aware that Harker University was financially committed to diversity as substantial funds were available for recruiting minorities at all levels. Concerned faculty, however, informed Cantor that there had been considerable difficulty with attracting minorities to the university in the past. Some reasons they noted were:

- minority faculty don't want to leave metropolitan areas to come to rural communities;
- there is no minority community in the town of Harker;
- minority faculty cost too much;
- the weather is too adverse for minorities in Harker; and
- qualified minority faculty are hard to find.

Perhaps these were all legitimate reasons; nevertheless, Dean Cantor knew many well-qualified minorities and was sure they would come to HU if asked. He decided to assist the faculty in attracting minorities to the campus by networking within the black and minority caucuses of various professional organizations in which he was a member. He also made available travel awards for HU faculty to visit doctoral degree programs on historically black campuses, and provided an updated listing of professional meetings and seminars well-attended by minority faculty so that HU faculty could attend for recruitment purposes.

Structural Barriers

Even though the college's policy supported minority representation on search committees, there were so few people of color on campus that, oftentimes, white women were the only minority representatives utilized. For this reason, it was not unusual for departments to invite people of color from other affiliated departments of the university to participate on their search committees. Dean Cantor encouraged this approach, seeing it as a matter of extending a professional courtesy to potential candidates and as a welcoming gesture to people of color.

In one instance that found Cantor strongly urging that a person of color from another department be invited to join a search committee, one of the committee members filed a grievance against him. Cantor was accused of "forcing" diversity and the Vice President of Academic Affairs advised Cantor that since deans at HU had no role to play in the faculty search process, he should not get involved. "After all," the Vice President stated, "faculty have the expertise in the discipline, not the dean."

Cultural Barriers

At a national conference for higher education, a colleague of Cantor's, Dr. Michael Cohen and his wife, Dr. Nancy Cohen, approached the dean to express their interests in two faculty positions at HU that they saw advertised in a popular journal. Nancy had recently received her Ph.D. in chemistry and Michael was a professor of

English at a small liberal arts college. Both were interested in relocating.

Cantor knew that HU's chemistry department did not have any women or minority faculty at the time and introduced Nancy to the Dean of Science and Technology, Dr. Edward Kimmel. Kimmel was pleased with this potential new hire, and invited Nancy to the campus. She was interviewed and offered the job within two weeks.

Meanwhile, proceeding with caution because of his last experience with a faculty search committee, Cantor pondered his options for introducing Michael Cohen to the English department at HU. Cantor decided to invite Michael to the campus as a lecturer, recalling an abbreviated process recently used by a fellow dean at HU to hire a minority faculty.

As Michael Cohen delivered his lecture, he was rudely interrupted by a senior African American faculty member who was not a member of the English department. He had been invited by a colleague. This visiting faculty openly challenged Cohen provoking a very confrontational exchange. The scene worked to confirm fears that African American males were hostile, aggressive and emotionally intense. It seemed the "contrived, on-site plant" had performed well to discredit the lecturer.

Weeks passed. Dean Cantor attempted to constitute a democratically elected departmental committee to confirm the appointment of Dr. Michael Cohen consistent with the model used by fellow deans at the university. For four months, the faculty resisted Cantor's efforts. Finally, both Nancy and Michael Cohen accepted positions at a more receptive and prestigious university.

Three more grievances were filed against Cantor, charging him with anti-union behavior. The Chancellor of the University System was pressured to hire an investigator to examine these serious charges. The system paid more than $9,000 for the investigation and formal report which were comprised of a series of charges and countercharges made by faculty. When asked why faculty supportive of Dean Cantor, or Cantor himself, were not interviewed in preparation for this report, the investigator said that the system only retained him to investigate claims of anti-union behavior, not to determine whether the dean had acted in good faith.

Conclusion

The fiscal climate at HU was optimal for recruiting minority faculty and staff members. However, the intolerant cultural and racial climates within the department hindered progress. At Harker University, white academic deans were able to make exceptions to hiring practices without being challenged by the faculty. At every turn, the dean of color was challenged.

While the faculty were able to invite an outside person of color to the department to influence the search process, albeit negatively, Dean Cantor could not share the same privilege. And even though other deans used expeditious routes to hire persons of color, Dean Cantor, over a four-month period, was inhibited in his efforts to implement the same procedure in his department.

Many African American deans in PWIs have similar experiences in which faculty are threatened by issues of race and ethnicity. These deans report constant harassment as they attempt to exercise their roles as leaders. Such behaviors and attitudinal problems act as serious barriers to progress especially if faculty take on gatekeeping functions as members of search committees and limit the number of minority candidates in the final pool. University policies and guidelines, which appear on the surface fair to all parties, are easily compromised and changed to meet personal ends.

Recommendations

Henry Frierson (1990) states that the success of minorities in the academic milieu rests with "knowing who you are and what you face." This philosophy is also expressed in a Chinese proverb which reads, "If you know the enemy and know yourself, you need not fear the result of a hundred battles. If you know yourself but not the enemy, for every victory gained you will also suffer defeat. And if you know neither the enemy nor yourself, you will succumb in every battle."

In addition to these prophecies, we suggest aspiring and current minority administrators:

- Have a realistic understanding of how one will be judged in comparison to white colleagues.

- Be aware of the institution's climate for diversity.

- Remember the academy is a mirror of society.

- Be clear on the expectations of one's role as a leader.

- Insist on a thorough orientation to the position for which one is hired.

- Disregard those who resist change and discourage progress from goal attainment.

- Keep the following primers by Harvey Mackay handy: *Beware the Naked Man Who Offers You His Shirt* and *Swim With the Sharks Without Being Eaten Alive.*

BIBLIOGRAPHY

Allen, B. P. & Niss, J. F. (1990, April). A chill in the college classroom? *Phi Delta Kappan,* 71, 607–609.

Baker, C. V. (ed.). (1989). The condition of education. *Postsecondary Education,* 2. Washington, DC: United States Department of Education.

Bates, P. & Wilson, T. (eds.). (1989). *Effective Schools: Critical Issues in the Education of Black Children.* Detroit, MI: National Alliance of Black School Educators.

Blanchard, F. A. (May 13, 1992). Combatting intentional bigotry and inadvertently racist acts. *Chronicle of Higher Education,* B1.

Carter, D. J. & Wilson, R. (1989). *Eighth Annual Status Report: Minorities in Education.* Washington, DC: American Council on Education.

Comer, J. P. (1988, November). Educating poor and minority children. *Scientific America,* 42–48.

Frierson, H. T., Jr. (1990). The situation of black educational researchers: Continuation of a crisis. *Educational Researcher,* 19 (2), 12–17.

Green, M. F. (ed.). (1989). *Minorities on Campus: A Handbook for Enhancing Diversity.* Washington, DC: American Council on Education.

Hidalgo, N. M., McDowell, C. L. & Siddle, E. V. (eds.). (1990). *Facing Racism in Education.* Cambridge, MA: Harvard Education Review.

Justus, J. B., Freitag, S. B. & Parker, L. L. (1987, Spring). *The University of California in the Twenty-First Century: Successful Approaches to Faculty Diversity.* Berkeley, CA: University of California Press.

Kropp, A. (April 22, 1992). Colleges must find ways to eradicate racial division. *Chronicle of Higher Education*, B3–4.

Mackay, H. (1990). *Beware the Naked Man Who Offers You His Shirt.* New York, NY: Morrow.

Mackay, H. (1988). *Swim With the Sharks Without Being Eaten Alive.* New York, NY: Morrow.

Otlinger, C. A. (ed.). (1989). *Higher Education Today: Facts in Brief.* Washington, DC: American Council on Education.

Pine, G. J. & Hilliard, A. G. (1990, April). Rx for racism: Imperatives for American's schools. *Phi Delta Kappan*, 71, 593–600.

Stanford University. (1989, March). *Building a Multiracial, Multicultural University Community: Final Report of the University Committee on Minority Issues.* Stanford, CA: Stanford University Press.

Strickland, G. & Holzman, L. (1989). Developing poor and minority children as leaders with the Barbara Taylor School educational model. *Journal of Negro Education*, 58, 383–398.

Tidwell, B. J. (1993). *The State of Black America.* New York, NY: National Urban League, Inc.

Trachtenberg, S. J. (1990, April). Multiculturalism can be taught only by multicultural people. *Phi Delta Kappa*, 71, 610–611.

University of Michigan. (1990, March). *The Michigan Mandate: A Strategic Linking of Academic Excellence and Social Diversity.* Dearborn, MI: University of Michigan.

Viadero, D. (1989, May). Schools witness a troubling revival of bigotry. *Education Week*, 8, 6.

Washington, V. & Harvey W. (1989). *Affirmative Rhetoric, Negative Action: African American and Hispanic Faculty at Predominantly White Institutions.* ASHE-ERIC Higher Education Report 2. Washington, DC: George Washington University.

Wilson, R. & Justiz, M. J. (1988). Minorities in higher education: Confronting a time bomb. *Educational Record,* 69, 8-15.

7

Dispelling Myths, Affecting Change: A Dominican Woman's Journey Through the Groves of Academe

DAISY COCCO DE FILIPPIS

Daisy Cocco De Filippis is Acting Associate Dean for Academic Affairs at York College (City University of New York) where she has taught language and literature in the Department of Foreign Languages since 1978. Dedicated to the inclusion of Dominican letters in North American literary circles, Dr. De Filippis is the author of numerous publications in this area.

Since 1960, there has been substantial growth in publications by women and about women that work to debunk myths regarding who women are and how they conduct themselves. Myths are defined as, "stories of unknown authorship, ostensibly with a historical basis but serving to explain a culture's customs, institutions and rites." In his modern interpretation of the roles of myths in academia, *Today's Myths and Tomorrow's Realities*, Richard M. Millard defines myths as the obstacles to be overcome as we achieve academic leadership in the twenty-first century. Women who have labored for some time in academe, as I have, recognize myths as "the stuff of which an institution's culture is made."

This essay explores two myths presented in Millard's work as they relate to my own experience. They are the relationship between underprepared and underachieving minority students and the liberal arts; and minority women in administrative positions. To enhance this examination, I offer my personal journey from faculty member to assistant dean at York College.

The College

York College was originally founded as Alpha College and located in northern Queens, New York, the population of which is suburban, white and upper middle class.

Today, York College is located in the heart of South Jamaica, Queens, and serves a predominantly minority and immigrant student body. In fact, Queens is the most ethnically diverse of New York's boroughs. Given this shift in the ethnicity of the student population, the evolution of the college is provided as a historical backdrop to show how myth-making occurs.

Myth: Underprepared and Underachieving Minority Students Will Benefit the Most from Career-Oriented Studies

York College, the fifth of the senior colleges of the City University of New York System was founded in 1967. The 1967-68 York College *Bulletin* tells of a college where lofty ideals preceded material and physical presence and a specific curricular design. Its founding members believed that "as a new institution, York College has a rare opportunity to try fresh approaches to old, old problems." Reading these lines and others like them in the *Bulletin* helps one relive, albeit vicariously, the energy and vitality of the founding group and their fervent belief that the college was meant to play an important role in contemporary, urban society.

This belief, apparently, was shared by administrators and others in the City University of New York system who projected:

> York College will grow and develop rapidly, but not in size beyond the point where it can maintain its dedication to excellence and its character as a community of persons. Enrollment projections are designed to prevent the impersonal, mass-production characteristics of many huge public institutions of higher learning.

Dedication to excellence and its character as a community of persons were at the heart of the York College enterprise and much thought was given to the philosophical framework that would guide the college as it developed. To aid in this, founding president, Dumont Kenny, established the York College Council on Academic Development. The council, funded by the Ford Foundation, consisted of a cadre of educators of national and international renown, including Mark Van Doren, Richard Peter McKeon and Rosemary Park Anastos. Members of the council served as consultants to the administration and faculty in a wide range of areas, one of which was curriculum development. In addition, members of the council agreed to give special lectures and seminars on a regular basis throughout the academic year. It seemed everything that would ensure the growth of a healthy and demanding intellectual life at the institution was in place prior to York College opening its doors to students.

To everyone's surprise, however, the curriculum proposed in the college's first *Bulletin* was far from being well thought out. The curricular descriptions consisted of brief recommendations for a "normal" freshman program and was comprised of courses in history, mathematics, literature and physical science; however, the listing of courses offered to students was limited to four courses in either French, German, Hebrew, Italian, Russian or Spanish; four courses in mathematics; and two courses in both literature and physical science. The inconsistency between courses offered and the recommended curriculum represents one of the many difficulties the college was to encounter that first year. Another was in terms of physical space.

Funding for the construction of the campus was not available until many years after its founding. There were difficulties in funding enough adjacent space to accommodate all offices. Consequently, offices for administration and academic departments were housed in different towns throughout Queens county. Classes were held in trailers in an area adjacent to a community college. Students did not receive the benefits of a "contained campus" site; and, as one can imagine, the academic environment was extremely disjointed, creating hardships for students and staff alike.

By the time the 1968–69 *Bulletin* went to print, the faculty had voted to support a rigorous liberal arts core curriculum which included the following requirements: English (nine credits), history (six credits), philosophy (six credits), fine and performing arts (four credits), behavioral sciences (six credits), mathematics (four credits), physical science (fourteen credits), foreign languages (six to fourteen credits), and physical education (two credits). In addition, the *Bulletin* listed ten programs for concentrated study in the liberal arts ranging from twenty-one to thirty-three required credits.

The curricular initiatives of the college's first years clearly articulated its mission as a small, liberal arts college designed to train academically competitive students. Curricular offerings were also enhanced by the creation of a "Wednesdays Program." This innovative program mandated that classes would not be scheduled on Wednesdays to give faculty and students the opportunity to go off-campus, into the urban environment of New York City, and gain hands-on experience in their respective fields of study.

Challenges to the Founding Vision

In 1969 it was established that York College would be located permanently in South Jamaica, Queens. The 1969–70 *Bulletin*, restating the college's mission, reads:

> …now designated to be located permanently in South Jamaica, Queens, York College is faced with the unique challenge—the challenge of

attempting to reverse the trends which have brought physical and social blight to an important area in the most important city in America. York College expects to play an appropriate role in meeting that challenge.

In comparing this mission statement to the college's founding statement (mentioned previously), a subtle change in tone is noted. Sobering expressions such as "attempting," "expects" and "appropriate" predominate. Additionally, the Wednesdays Program was discarded and the York College Council on Academic Development no longer existed. In fact, the founding president resigned. He felt he had lost the political struggle over the mission of the college.

In the seventies, institutions nationwide dropped stringent liberal arts core curricula from their offerings, only to have them reinstated a few years later after it was determined these cores were an important part of a student's education. At York College, this was not the case. Instead, there were many heated debates on campus regarding the formulation of a new core curriculum which would best address the needs of students. At a highly emotional faculty meeting, the acting president signaled its end by tearing the *Bulletin* in half as he proclaimed, "The trivium and the quadrivium ain't where it's at!" Amused philosophers, having lost the good fight, retained their good spirits long enough to wonder uncharitably if the man knew what the trivium and quadrivium were.

The 1972–73 *Bulletin* shows a change in the core curriculum. There were new general requirements that called for eight to eleven credits in core courses, and thirty-two to thirty-three credits in area requirements. The rigorous requirements in foreign languages, humanities and natural sciences were reduced to accommodate the credits required for new professional programs which ballooned to as many as sixty-one credits. This was a far cry from the twenty-one to thirty-three credit spread proposed at the college's inception. In addition, the curriculum change was an affirmation of an emerging mindset that professed the liberal arts as nonfunctional in a college such as York College. These changes remained in place for nearly twenty years.

In January of 1991, the second president of York College retired after twenty years of service. At this time, there were not any women in positions at the dean's level or above. There were, however, three African American men in cabinet positions. To what extent the lack of women and minority administrators effected the direction York College had assumed is hard to determine. Nevertheless, the fact that the college's institutional culture took a significant turn is quite clear.

The liberal arts curriculum heralded and supported by the founding faculty was subsumed by one abundant in professional programs. The possibility of maintaining a rigorous liberal arts curriculum while simultaneously developing professional programs to respond to the needs and pressures of the labor market was not supported nor seriously considered. Hence, the myth that liberal arts and liberal studies should not be provided to "underprepared and underachieving" minority students prevailed. Unfortunately, this myth still prevails in many American institutions of higher education.

Myth: Women, Particularly Minority Women, are Incapable of Being Effective Leaders in Academe

When I arrived at York College in 1978, I was a doctoral student working on my dissertation. I was pleased to discover that the place I was to call "work" was a warm, welcoming place—a home away from home. Over time I learned the closeness I felt at work was based on the department's vision of itself as a sort of island unto itself, barely hanging on at a time of shrinking resources and in an environment that the liberal arts, particularly foreign languages, were not supported by either academic requirements or resources.

In hindsight, I can see that the representation, or perhaps I should say underrepresentation, of cultural diversity in traditional liberal arts fields, such as history and English, mirrors the inequality that exists in institutions of higher learning in this country. Horror stories abound. It suffices here to recall Hillis Miller's remarks, "I believe in the established canon of English and American literature and in the validity of the concept of privileged texts. I think it is more important to read Spenser, Shakespeare or Milton than to read Borges in translation, or even, to say the truth, Virginia Woolf." The choice of authors Miller includes in his "less important than" category is neither casual nor innocent. Both Woolf and Borges enjoy reputations which far exceed those of most female authors and Latin American authors, respectively. In Miller's view, all others are unacceptable, less important, inferior. This view, apparently, is shared by many of his colleagues. A perusal of any Modern Language Association (MLA) conference program in recent years will confirm that language departments have certainly been relegated to the realm of the *other* (i.e., less than).

These concerns, however, were not part of the world as I knew it when I first came to York College. Then, I felt privileged to be able to teach and very fortunate to get paid for work I so thoroughly enjoyed. Teaching at York College was also emotionally rewarding because it tapped into my interpretation of Latin American womanhood, and supplied me with the unique opportunity to touch and change the lives of students who so closely resembled me. Furthermore, as a member of a culture that professed that women should not speak out in public, teaching at York College helped me reach a compromise between my role as a Hispanic woman and my role as an academic and professional.

I acquired a sense of fulfillment, based perhaps on my development of what North American writer, Tillie Olsen, refers to as "woman's infinite capacity to tend to the needs of others." I became a favorite in the department because of my ability to deal with details, such as class schedules, uniform syllabi, memoranda, etc. I had a knack for organizing poetry contests and trips to the theater, and establishing organizations and programs like a peer tutoring program, a Spanish journal and an honor society. During this time, my status as the only minority, full-time person employed in the department had never affected my ability to achieve professional goals. As I prepared to present myself for tenure and promotion, however, this changed. It seemed as though this step towards advancement gave voice to the yet unsaid, albeit existing myth: As a professional, I was acceptable as a working underling but not as an equal.

To combat this myth, I quite simply persevered. I submitted for both considerations well aware that my work in terms of scholarship, student support activities and service to the college could not possibly be overlooked; and I was right. I was elected chairperson of the faculty caucus. In the absence of exemplary models of female leadership, I was judged by masculine traits and expected to perform by men's standards. I had to teach myself how to overlook public opinion; and, believe me, as a woman from a culture that values public opinion to the extent that *honra* (honor) is recognized as a quality bestowed upon one by one's peers, this was not an easy task. In doing this, it helped me to be aware that it is common for women who are in the public arena to be subjected to hostility and stereotyping based on a double standard and resulting in the following presumptions:

He's confident...She's conceited.

He's enthusiastic...She's emotional.

He's not afraid to say what he thinks...She's difficult to work for.

He follows through...She doesn't know when to quit.

He's firm...She's stubborn.

He's an authority...She's a tyrant.

(Pearsall, 1986)

Perhaps the most important step I took in establishing myself as an equal at York College, however, was to make the effort and take the time to build solid, professional relationships with colleagues. To accomplish this, I made myself visible in other departments across campus by running for, and subsequently being elected as, a senator in the faculty caucus and the York College Senate. As one of only two elected representatives from my department, my appointment indicated that I was making progress in my quest to dispel myths.

In the Summer of 1990, this quest was fully realized. As one of the many concerned faculty on campus, I had the opportunity to work on revising the general curriculum to include diversity with twenty-five colleagues from different backgrounds and academic disciplines. The group gathered once a week to discuss, plan and draft curriculum proposals which would change the culture of the college and the academic preparation of our students. To enhance our experience, we agreed to bring food and drink from our own cultures. It was a communion of spirits seldom encountered in an environment traditionally hostile to multiculturalism. It was evident that the time had come for the campus to embrace change.

Despite enduring hostility in some quarters, my colleagues began to understand that multiculturalism did not threaten traditional Western values, but rather expanded the concept of culture. Further, they saw multiculturalism as an enrichment of the educational experience our students receive. However, it was not until I understood the necessity of "converting" one of the more conservative and traditional members of the college "community" to a supporter of our cause and an ambassador of goodwill from the Multicultural Committee that colleagues accepted the validity of what I, as caucus leader and co-chair of the Multicultural Committee, was advocating. This relationship, begun for political expediency on both of our parts, has since blossomed into a solid and cherished friendship.

This experience convinced me that the liberal arts, when embraced by a Hispanic woman and presented in the form of philosophies, cultures and literatures by and about nondominant groups, are deemed suspect. For these efforts to be validated, it was necessary to have the initiative endorsed and presented by a spokesman for traditional values who was also a member of the community of abused kindred spirits. Having made this allegiance and received the approval of the insiders within the community of scholars, the multicultural curriculum was passed to include a general core with foreign languages. The majority of my colleagues in the senate also approved the proposal.

In effect, this new core curriculum for York College in the 1990s was a much more substantial and comprehensive general education experience than the curriculum required during the heyday of the liberal arts at York College. The

1991 *Bulletin* includes the following core distribution: English writing, English literature, speech, foreign languages (three semesters), cultural diversity (two courses out of four offered), Western civilization, history or philosophy, three courses from the behavioral sciences, four courses in mathematics and sciences (including a lab course), and one course in the fine and performing arts.

Progress marched on at York College with the arrival of its third president, an African American female, and my subsequent appointment to the position of acting assistant dean for curriculum and faculty development. I had decided that the time had come to join an administrative team which truly represented the rainbow coalition of educators—a coalition much needed in this country. Profound and lasting changes on campus were the result of this decision.

I have been able to work with colleagues to assure the construction of a Faculty Resource Center where discourse between colleagues interested in bettering York College can be nurtured and supported. I have facilitated, with the leadership and kind interests of both the president and the American Association for Higher Education, the development of faculty portfolios to assist in decisions regarding reappointment, tenure and promotion. Colleagues are now able to document their contributions to the college using the portfolio approach and their efforts have been rewarded as the rewards system of the college has changed to include a discourse about the merit of the scholarship of teaching.

I have also participated with colleagues in faculty training sessions designed to facilitate the implementation of the cultural diversity component of the core curriculum. Courses such as "Understanding Cultural Diversity in the United States" as well as humanities courses on the Haitian, Hispanic and Asian experience have been incorporated into the curriculum. Also, there are new language introductory offerings in Swahili, Creole, Chinese and Greek. More often than not, these offerings are oversubscribed by York College students.

CONCLUSIONS

York College's history of curriculum development and implementation presents a shying away from the teaching of liberal arts as the college's mission changed from educating middle class students to an increasingly minority student population. Although the college has continued to define itself as a liberal arts institution, its limited resources have been allocated to support professional career programs.

Statistics indicate that York College has a very low retention rate. It is clear, then, that the professional programs route has not yielded the desired results as far as the college's mission to educate and aid in the restoration of an important, depleted area is concerned. In addition, the Board of Trustees approved a revised core curriculum which addresses the need to reintroduce a strong general education preparation for students at York College. At the same time, the university declared financial exigency, and retrenchment was declared at the college. In a climate of fiscal constraint, it is difficult to implement a general education curriculum which redresses accumulated deficiencies. In the face of these challenges, will urban students again lose the opportunity to pursue a career in the liberal arts? As indicated earlier by course oversubscriptions, minority students are interested in the liberal arts if given the opportunity. I believe that if allowed to grow, the liberal arts will flourish in South Jamaica.

On a more personal level, my experience at York College, while difficult at times, has fostered my growth in ways I never expected or thought were within my grasp. I have learned to take the nurturing expected of women in my culture and move it to the sphere of public life and participation. I write these pages with the ambition of shedding some light on the very complex issue of diversity in American educational institutions. I hope that my words will encourage other Hispanic women to come out of their offices and undertake the road to self-expression and participation in the activities of their institutions. I also hope that colleagues of other cultures will reexamine behaviors, expectations and preconceived notions regarding those different from the dominant group.

In closing, I offer the well-founded observation that no one moves forward in life without the mentoring and support of her or his peers and supervisors. It is those colleagues who share with me a dream guided not by gender and race, but solid scholarship, a sense of fairness and a desire to recognize the contributions of all cultures that affect change. To quote New York Mayor David Dinkins, it is the "wonderful mosaic of humanity" that defines what it means to be an American.

BIBLIOGRAPHY

Eble, K. E. (1977). *The Art of Administration: A Guide for Academic Administrators*. San Francisco, CA: Jossey-Bass.

Fisher, R., et al. (1991). *Getting to Yes 2/e*. New York, NY: Penguin Books.

Flores, A. & Flores, K. (eds.). (1986). *The Defiant Muse: Hispanic Feminists from the Middle Ages to the Present*. New York, NY: Feminist Press.

Green, M. F. (ed.). (1989). *Minorities on Campus: A Handbook for Enhancing Diversity.* Washington, DC: American Council on Education.

Herrera-Sobek, M., et al. (eds.). (1989). *Chicana Creativity and Criticism: Charting New Frontiers in American Literature.* Houston, TX: Arte Publico Press.

Millard, R. M. (1991). *Today's Myths and Tomorrow's Realities: Overcoming Obstacles to Academic Leadership in the 21st Century.* San Francisco, CA: Jossey-Bass.

Olsen, T. (1978). *Silences 3/e.* New York, NY: Delacorte Press.

Pearsall, M. (ed.) (1986). *Women and Values: Readings in Recent Feminist Philosophy.* Belmont, CA: Wadsworth Publishing Co.

York College Bulletin. (1967–1992). The City University of New York.

8

Recruitment and Retention of Minority Faculty and Students on Historically White Campuses

DAVID W. WILLIAMS

David W. Williams is Provost and Vice President for Academic Affairs, as well as Professor of Education, at Metropolitan State College of Denver. Dr. Williams received his Ph.D. in Student Development from The Ohio State University. He has served as Vice Chancellor for Academic Affairs, Illinois Board of Regents; Vice President for Academic Affairs, Fort Valley State College; and President, Allen University. He is active in numerous professional and community organizations.

African American, Hispanic American, Native American and Asian American faculty often feel that the commitment of higher education to faculty diversification is shallow. Their experiences as new faculty members on campus reflect a shift in interest from their development as quality professionals to an interest in the "numbers game." It appears that most minority faculty are recruited principally to upgrade institutional data for compliance reporting purposes. Few reap the benefits of a long-term residence on a historically white campus as respected members of the academy.

As evidenced in exit interviews, faculty of color share painful recollections of their survival in hostile camps. Compared to their majority group peers, opportunities for advancement in faculty rank are qualitatively inferior. Faculty of color carry disproportionately high teaching, advising and service loads; their research and scholarly activities are undervalued; lip-service is given to their despondent cries for assistance with culturally-generic problems; and they are cut off from a range of supportive services within their academic departments as well as within their own disciplines. Victimized by subtle but powerful ethnic, gender and/or sexual harassment, they feel isolated and alienated. These feelings adversely affect their personal well-being in addition to their professional performance.

MINORITIES IN HIGHER EDUCATION

In 1986–1987, only eleven percent of Ph.D. recipients were minorities. In all postsecondary institutions, the minority presence was just ten percent (Crews, 1990). If higher education institutions are to compete successfully for these small-sized talent pools, then serious attention has to be given to creating campus climates that are more favorable to minority retention.

Changing campus climate means changing behaviors that are set by rites, rituals, and rewards of the academy. Charles Moody, Vice Provost of Academic Affairs at the University of Michigan, often states, "The climate [suggests] whatever minority candidates have isn't needed and whatever they don't have is exactly what is needed...[it is difficult] for beneficiaries of racism to be able to see racism" (Anderson, 1991). He recommends conducting a thorough assessment of campus climate using the perspective of minority students and alumni. Moody believes that the use of student voices, particularly minority student voices, is an effective means of removing institutional blindness to racist acts.

Most faculty of color leave historically white institutions (HWIs) before the end of their probationary periods. They do not choose to struggle to gain promotion and tenure in extremely hostile environments. Among all minorities, African American faculty have the lowest retention and promotion rates in academia (Association of American Colleges, 1988). Women's experiences are similar. According to a study conducted in the University of Wisconsin System, women throughout the system leave at a higher rate than men (University of Wisconsin, 1990); and of these women, minority women leave at the highest rate. Should the present rate of attrition continue, the Wisconsin study projects it will need to replace up to thirty-eight percent of its minority faculty between now and the year 2000 to maintain its current level of diversity. For historically white institutions to stabilize the retention of minority faculty, particularly African American faculty, three factors should be considered: 1) the environment, 2) the department, and 3) sources of daily interactions.

THE ENVIRONMENT

Environmentally troubled academic departments operate on the premise that the knowledge they produce and the administrative practices they construct and implement are perfectly rational, neutral and objective. The cultural context exists in a space that appears to be outside the pervasive forces of ethnic and gender bias. Diversity is typically regarded as a threat to the quality of the department's academic environment as well as an intrusion on administrative sovereignty. Diversity is operationalized as access to a political windfall of resources that otherwise would not be available. When implemented, diversity is viewed as an access point to a political windfall of resources that otherwise would not have to be dealt with. No critical self-examination takes place within the troubled departmental environment. In fact, the department's philosophy may be: "We don't need rules; we trust us" (Shaw, 1991).

Troubled environments reduce the lengthy challenges of diversity to the single problem of hiring "their black" or "their women" from an inadequate labor pool. Affirmative action ends, in fact, with the act of hiring. The newly hired person is given the duty to "get along with others," to "overcome 'skewed' perceptions," to "learn how to be 'rational and neutral,'" and to "accept criticism 'without protest'" (Blackwell, 1990).

The Department

Lest we look for Utopia, let it be understood that no department, however supportive, can insulate women and other minority faculty from bias. As mentioned earlier, departments generally assign a disproportionately large amount of teaching to women or foster a rigid "property rights" approach to the assignment of upper-level courses. Many minority faculty report difficulty in gaining support from members of curricular review committees or their own department for the inclusion of courses and/or new programs pertaining to their own ethnicity. Research and publications related to the contributions and scholarships of people of color are also devalued in the promotion and tenure process. Additionally, the retention process does not grant minority faculty any extra consideration for the enormous time spent beyond advisement and office hours facilitating the socialization of minority students on campus; for this is time which could otherwise be spent in *scholarly* pursuits.

Some departments reserve travel support and faculty development opportunities for senior tenured professors. When minority faculty protest the imbalance in resource distributions, retaliations are made later at tenure or promotion time. Angered senior faculty cite examples of poor interpersonal skills, failure to adjust, or lack of cooperation with well-established departmental policies as grounds not to retain "contentious" minority faculty. In desperation, faculty of color leave these white halls of ivy for safer havens on campuses which advocate principles more consonant with their own backgrounds, training and ethnicity.

Daily Interactions

Mentoring

One of the best ways for a faculty member or administrator to show acceptance of minority protégés is to "break bread with them." Mentoring provides one such opportunity. As a survival strategy for minority faculty, the process of mentoring pairs incoming minority faculty with senior faculty, who may or may not be in the same department, in relationships which provide insight and support to both partners. Charles Vert Willie, Harvard School of Education professor, believes that the first principle of successful mentoring is "...to accept that fact that the minority is unlike the majority. Whenever the minority feels that he or she has to forget where he/she came from and act like someone who he or she is not, that person is in trouble" (Sands, Parson & Duane, 1991).

Mentoring provides a sense of familiarity and contributes to the building of friendships. The partnership between the mentor and the protégé determines the scope of the relationship. Interactions may vary from telephone conversations and meetings for morning coffee to more extended relationships involving family dinners or other outings. An effective mentor will spend informal time with the partner and be willing to share all the necessary ingredients for success. When faculty mentor other faculty within the same department, however, the nature of the relationship takes on a more complex shape. Those who are mentored by colleagues put themselves in an unequal and vulnerable position in relation to the person who, sometime in the future, may be making decisions about their tenure and promotion. In view of the sensitive issues that faculty-faculty mentorships portend, personal relationships may be somewhat more constrained than those formed in faculty-student relationships. Regardless of the nature of the mentor-protégé relationship, for the retention of minority faculty to become a reality, majority administrators, faculty, staff and students must be prepared to give minority faculty the same benefits of doubt or promise given to white candidates and faculty. Studies suggest that the search for competence and potential should transcend racial, ethnic and gender lines (Clay, 1990).

Alienating Behaviors

Oftentimes, minority faculty who struggle to survive in nonsupportive environments recall being greeted warmly at hiring. Over time, this warm environment turns cool and eventually gives way to one of silence and perhaps even isolation. At first, most minority faculty will deny that racism is at the base of this environmental turn because it contrasts starkly with the very beneficent receptions they received on campus. Many blame themselves for the onset of problems and, as they intensify, most try to reach out to senior faculty members, chairs, or both. This approach elicits one of four reactions:

- they are told that they are the problem;
- they are told that the problem is in their heads and should try harder to "fit in";
- they are unable to engage anyone in meaningful dialogue about their problems; and
- they receive sincere promises for assistance that never materialize or that fail to address the root of the problem.

That these reactions subsist in institutions across the country affirm and reaffirm the need to "...celebrate women and minorities [so that] they [can] take their rightful places as faculty members, as administrators, as members of boards of trustees, and as members of various programs—both social and cultural" (Wiley, 1990). In doing so, diversity across college and university campuses will, at long last, be enabled to flourish.

MEANS FOR PROMOTING FACULTY DIVERSITY: A CASE STUDY

Metropolitan State College of Denver

In an effort to improve its campus climate for diversity, Metropolitan State College of Denver developed three initiatives during the Fall of 1990: the Target of Opportunity Program (TOP), the Minority Faculty Recruitment Incentive Program (MFRIP), and the New Faculty Mentoring Program (NFMP). These initiatives were designed to increase the number of women and minority administrators, to attract national and international faculty of distinction to the campus, and to retain quality minority faculty. The programs do not supersede established affirmative action screening and selection processes; rather they provide alternative approaches to diversify Metropolitan State College of Denver's faculty, staff and administration.

Target of Opportunity Program (TOP)

This program provides flexible, less time-consuming recruiting and hiring procedures, as well as additional resources for administrators to draw upon in their search new hires. Essentially, TOP provides for and expedites the search for and subsequent hiring of: a) women and ethnic minority faculty when there is either an underutilization of a particular protected group or when there is a special need for representation of a particular protected group;

b) nationally and/or internationally recognized minority faculty when the opportunity presents itself; and c) women and minority administrators when there is either underutilization of a protected class or a special need for representation of a protected class within a particular academic unit.

Minority Faculty Recruitment Incentive Program (MFRIP)

This program allows academic departments that are experiencing reasonably stable or slow growth in enrollments to aggressively recruit minority candidates. MFRIP also provides support for professional development. That is, faculty interested in pursuing graduate studies leading to a terminal degree or to a different specialization may be supported through this initiative.

In this program, the vice president of academic affairs provides incentive awards of $5,000 to any minority faculty accepting promotion to a tenure-track position. There is, however, a limit of one such development award per department. Also, the incentive award must be provided in the fall semester of the year preceding the initial appointment, e.g. a development award would be made in the Fall of 1992 for an appointment commencing in the Fall of 1993.

Minority faculty receiving the academic development awards are eligible for a maximum of $8,000 in financial support over a period not to exceed five years. These funds may be used for tuition reimbursement, released time, sabbatical leave and/or other special conditions defined in the contract. Those faculty who complete their terminal degree requirements and who receive satisfactory evaluations are offered tenure-track positions at the college.

The New Faculty Mentoring Program (NFMP)

This program grew out of a need to develop a cadre of committed, resourceful and qualified new faculty, especially from the ranks of protected groups such as the physically impaired, women, African Americans, Native Americans, Asian Americans and Hispanic Americans. The program's objectives are to assist new faculty, to provide new faculty with a peer support network, and to ensure them a smooth progression through the retention, tenure and promotion process. The program requires all incoming faculty to be advised of its requirements during recruitment.

NFMP is unit-based with each dean having full responsibility for his or her establishment and operation. The dean and department chair pair incoming faculty with a suitable veteran faculty member. Preferably, this veteran faculty member is a colleague within the same department as the incoming faculty. Faculty from outside the department who share the incoming faculty's area of interest and teaching/job-related assignment are suitable for pairing as well. The responsibilities of these mentors are to give academic support, to provide information about the campus and other faculty support services, and to supply constructive advice as requested or needed.

Tangible Results

As of 1992–93, eighteen ethnic minority faculty members were hired by the college in various academic departments through the Minority Faculty Recruitment Incentive Program and the Target of Opportunity Program. Fourteen of these new hires were women, seven of whom were ethnic minorities. During the first year with these programs, eleven percent of the 363 full-time instructional faculty employed during the 1990–91 academic year were ethnic females and over fourteen percent were ethnic males. It is not known what the impact of the NFMP has had on the retention of minority faculty; time, of course, will tell.

The college recognizes the need to continue enhancing current efforts to acquire and retain qualified minorities. To this end, the Office of the Provost and Vice President for Academic Affairs at the college has submitted a proposal to the Department of Education requesting funds for initiating a résumé depository and starting a training program for developing hiring guidelines for institutions in the region. The intent is to make available to participating regional institutions résumés from qualified minorities in any geographic location.

CONCLUSION

America has an important choice to make: adopt and reconcile its differing peoples and cultural traditions or splinter into cultural and social apartheid. Facilitating diversity is not only the right and proper course—it is the sensible thing to do. The central mission of undergraduate education is to prepare students to live in the world as it is and will be. Students must encounter a pluralistic mix of fellow students—to include people with disabilities, the minority-majority, internationals and others. Exclusivity is not excellence. Institutions will only achieve excellence through diversity.

Recommendations

Historically White Campuses. To retain minority faculty on historically white campuses, campus leaders must demonstrate more seriously their interest in cultivating a community of believers who value and welcome the differences people of color bring to the academy. Aggressive leadership is a prerequisite for change. It can overcome obstacles at all levels while encouraging equity from the grassroots. Presidents and chief academic officers must provide the leadership through systematic planning and the formulation of comprehensive strategies and evaluations. The goal of these initiatives should be that of assuring accountability in keeping the issue of minority retention continuously before the eyes of the academic community. Ultimately, a degree of comfort in the environment which will support social and intellectual interactions where stereotypes are questioned and where opportunities are provided for others to learn more about different cultures must be achieved.

Majority Faculty Responsibility. The responsibility to celebrate multiculturalism in its diverse forms must be accepted fully by majority faculty. Minority faculty must be recognized for their intellectual expertise in the areas of curriculum proposals or new programs; for their visions charted as alternative ways of conducting business and asking questions; and for their scholarship which may be as centered on the traditional as on other world perspectives. Faculty, as human academicians, should also assume full responsibility for assisting minority faculty with their transitions to campus life.

Coloring the Halls of Ivy. Coloring the halls of ivy holds the potential for releasing creative energies in untold proportions. Through exposure to the *other*, fear will dissipate and appreciation and respect will follow. For Metropolitan State College of Denver, initiatives in regard to coloring its halls are continuous.

Bibliography

Abid-Nader, J. (1991, March). Strategies for motivating minority students. *Phi Delta Kappan,* 72, 546–549.

Anderson, J. A. (1991, January). The politics of retention: Rhetoric vs. reality. *Black Issues in Higher Education,* 7 (24), 116.

Auster, C. J. & McClelland, K. E. (1990, Nov/Dec). Public platitudes and hidden tensions: Racial climates at predominantly white liberal arts colleges. *Journal of Higher Education,* 62 (6), 607–642.

Bennett, C. (1991, March). Toward a multicultural curriculum. *American Association for Higher Education Black Caucus,* 1 (3), 1–4.

Blackwell, J. E. (1990, June). Operationalizing faculty diversity. *American Association Bulletin,* 8–9.

Canclatore, J. (1991, January). Recruitment and retention: What works. *Black Issues in Higher Education,* 7, 40–42.

Carter, D. & Chandler, A. (1991, April). Fostering a multicultural curriculum: Principles for presidents. *American Association of State Colleges and Universities,* 2–8.

Clay, C. A. (1990, Summer). Creating an affirming climate. *Metropolitan Universities: An International Forum,* 61 (2), 41–51.

Crews, A. C. (1990, December). Needed: Real agents for change. *Black Issues in Higher Education,* 7 (21), 72.

Duane, J., Parson, L. A. & Sands, R. G. (1991, Mar/Apr). Faculty mentoring faculty in a public university. *The Journal of Higher Education,* 62 (2), 176–193.

Finn, C. E., Jr. (1990, July). Point of view. *The Chronicle of Higher Education,* 36, A40.

Leo, J. (1990, November). A fringe history of the world. *U. S. News and World Report,* 109 (12), 25–26.

Levitz, R. & Noel, L. (1990, Summer). The retention challenge: It can be met. *Metropolitan Universities: An International Forum,* 1 (2), 31–39.

Milne, J. & Priest, D. (1991, Winter/Spring). A next step in student retention: Academic advising. *Journal for Higher Education Management,* 7, 36–37.

Shaw, K. (1991, Winter). Diversity on campus: Welcoming new members. *Educational Record,* 72, 6–13.

Wiley, E., III. (1990, December). How deep is the stated commitment to diversity? *Black Issues in Higher Education,* 7 (21), 1,6-7.

9

Recruitment, Retention and Graduation of African American and Other Minority Students

DAVID W. WILLIAMS

Futuristic population trends indicate that by the end of the twentieth century, the African American population will have increased by twelve percent. Likewise, Asian populations are predicted to increase by twenty-two percent and Hispanic populations by twenty-one percent. White American populations, however, are to increase by only two percent. Within a generation, nonwhites will become the majority group. With this "browning of America," everything in society will be altered, from politics and industry to values, culture and education.

It seems changes in the law and attitudinal changes toward people of color have "significantly"improved college enrollment of minorities in predominantly white institutions. Also, aggressive efforts made by many institutions in terms of "affirmative action" seem to have removed discriminatory barriers on behalf of these traditionally excluded groups.

If this is so, then why is all *still* not well in academe? Why are incidents involving racism and racially motivated violence on college campuses increasing? And why are these institutions unable to retain and graduate the African American students they work so hard to recruit?

Minority students are often met with serious barriers, consisting of feelings of isolation, loneliness, dissonance and racially-motivated victimization, which inhibit their academic success on predominantly white campuses. To avoid many of these insecurities, some African American students choose to enroll in or transfer to historically black institutions where they can benefit from a more supportive social and academic environment. However, this course of action does not address the problem at hand. Rather, it circumvents it.

The retention of minorities in predominantly white institutions depends on the relationship between the administration and students. There should be support systems to assure that the African American student moves from general studies courses into more specific courses of study which complement the student's career interests. In other words, the institution should actively guide the student to graduating with a marketable degree.

On most campuses, retention efforts and programs are as varied as the institutions from which they emanate. Success in such programs is also defined vicariously. What appears to underscore all approaches, though, is the degree of training and expertise of those who develop and implement these programs. Since there is no formal training regimen from which retention specialists can draw, there is also no agreed upon method of assessment for program efficiency. When at-risk students, students of color and students from other diverse groups perform poorly in their studies, they are often held accountable for this outcome. It seems as though these students should be spared blame until retention programs, their staff and administrators have demonstrated excellence, or at least a functional knowledge base from which they operate. Further, because there is a direct correlation between quality academic advising programs and improved retention rates, it is critical for institutions to provide adequate financial support for academic advising programs. Students will be the primary beneficiaries of these efforts.

Academic advising can be a deterrent to attrition and a major step toward increasing the retention rate. Compassionate and pointed academic advising presents students with options and choices regarding their future while making clear the institutional regulations and requirements. There are a number of creative programs institutions can initiate to assure the successful matriculation of minorities in predominantly white institutions. Each of these programs must be comprehensive, spearheaded by the leadership and owned by the entire campus in order to accomplish established goals and objectives. Mentoring, orientation, peer advising, academic advising, and tutoring are but a few approaches to successful recruitment, retention and graduation. The plan must include recommendations, resources, assignment of responsibilities, and an evaluation process.

Metropolitan State College of Denver (MSCD) continues to demonstrate a strong commitment to minority students in the areas of recruitment, retention and graduation. In addition to the traditional programs available to serve students, several creative initiatives have been developed to further support the college's commitment.

RECRUITMENT

Project Excel. One such initiative, Project Excel, is a major early-outreach partnership between the Office of Admissions and Records at the college and the Denver Public School System. The main goal of this partnership is to expand the pool of academically qualified minority students entering higher education. Project Excel accesses information and assistance to high school students interested in pursuing a college education via ten current MSCD students, known as STARs (Student Tour and Admissions Representatives). Each STAR is assigned to a high school and works closely with the high school counselors, faculty and staff to:

1. Increase students' knowledge of the appropriate high school courses to take for adequate college preparation.

2. Enhance students' performance on college entrance

exams and writing samples by providing tutorial assistance and study skills seminars.

3. Improve students' understanding about higher education opportunities, admissions requirements and financial aid resources by offering workshops on choosing a college.

4. Prepare students for college life by introducing effective organization and time management skills in the classroom.

Special activities for high school sophomores, juniors and seniors are an integral part of the program with many events taking place on the college campus. Included in these activities is a shadowing experience in chosen career areas.

Summer Bridge Program. The Summer Bridge Program is a cooperative program between the Community College of Denver and Metropolitan State College of Denver designed to prepare high school students for entry into college by building on their academic, career, personal and social skills.

Summer Bridge participants carry six credit hours (two required courses) during the ten week program. One of the education courses, titled "Planning for Success," highlights the importance of time management for first-year students while providing models for study techniques and leadership skills. The second required course, which can be in either reading or math, emphasizes strengthening the mastery level of specific foundation skills. A preprogram assessment of the student-participants facilitates academic advising. Additionally, there is a four day college sampling session allowing each participant to rotate through eight different career/subject areas. Students are provided the opportunity to engage in discourse with faculty and counselors at the college. Numerous recreational and cocurricular activities are offered to student-participants throughout the summer.

ORIENTATION FOR MINORITY POPULATIONS

Orientation should be a two day event held after students have been assessed. The program should include minority and majority faculty representatives, support services staff, student organization representatives and other interested personnel.

Workshop activities should include college survival skills such as time management, budgeting for college (i.e., money management), resource familiarization, college terminology familiarization, career options, faculty/student relationships, etc. Minority faculty could have small group discussions with students and any attending parents. Student organizations could conduct workshops on student life to include assistance with registration, scheduling and textbook purchasing, as well as campus tours.

RETENTION

The Student Development Center. In addition to recruitment initiatives, Metropolitan State College of Denver established a Student Development Center to assist in improving the academic and intellectual achievements of students. Essentially, the center provides comprehensive and individualized services that promote retention and increase graduation rates, particularly in traditionally underrepresented student populations. Academic and personal counseling, assistance with the transition from high school to college, leadership development, advocacy, multicultural programs and activities, and support groups for various populations such as women, single parents and people of color are some of the arenas in which the center exerts itself.

The center engages community leaders and agencies to assist with the development of resources, such as employment and housing opportunities, to meet the needs of students. Equally important is the implementation of a four-day, mandatory sensitivity and diversity training workshop. This is executed in collaboration with local business and industry to increase employee social and cultural awareness, empowering them to deliver better and more functional services.

The Road to Success. This mentoring program is a college-wide initiative administered by the center and cosponsored by Student Support Services. The goal of the program is to strengthen the relationship between the administration and faculty, and students, by providing a more nurturing environment. Faculty act as role models for their students and work to become more involved in a students' academic development and subsequent success. A support group for mentors and an advisory board are additional components to the program. Also, a biweekly article appears in *The Metropolitan*, the school newspaper, featuring the outcomes and the benefits of student-mentor relationships, as well as the advantages accompanying the diversity of the educational community at MSCD.

The First-Year Program. Available to all first-year students, this successful program offers intensive advising, course selection guidance and academic monitoring throughout students' first year in college. Students engage in self-reflection regarding their attitudes toward higher education, as well as participate in reading and writing exercises focusing on relevant social issues. The program furnishes an environment in which problem-solving, creativity and peer interaction are encouraged.

Conclusion

There is a wealth of information concerning successful approaches to retention available to institutional leaders committed to retaining and graduating minority students. It is important to remember, however, that commitment begins with the courage to ask the tough questions, to engage in introspective assessment and to implement structural changes at all levels as the need arises. To those whose interests are in the pursuit of a culturally diverse, intellectually stimulating and inviting campus climate, I offer the following suggestions in the areas of recruitment and retention.

Recruitment

- Begin precollegiate activities for minority students as early as the eighth grade. Summer institutes for eighth through twelfth grade students provides a continuum to academic and career/college awareness activities, thus strengthening the college preparation for traditionally underrepresented populations. Sessions should be taught by current faculty members. Teacher education could utilize this effort for curriculum development, teacher preparation, and training of how to work with minority populations.

- Encourage academic departments to design summer institutes and provide intensive instruction for high school seniors and first-year college students in the areas of math, science, social sciences and English.

- Provide employment opportunities on campus for students to further expose them to campus life. Additionally, all such students should have mentors, being sure to include minority mentors.

- Promote cultural activities and celebrations during designated holidays (i.e., African American History month, Martin Luther King's birthday, *Cinco de Mayo*, Chinese New Year, etc.), thus providing ideal opportunities to bring high school seniors and their parents to the campus. During these visits, families can be provided with information about campus life and the institution can be recognized for its interests in diversity. Faculty and student groups should design these programs.

Retention

- Seek and utilize corporate sponsorship and scholarships. Minority students need more exposure to the "world of work" through internships and other experiences.

- Promote institutional change. Institutions need to move away from the deficit model and be more proactive in their approach to serving minority students. All minority students are not "underprepared," "deprived" or "different."

- Provide cultural sensitivity training and activities. This is of paramount importance.

- Institutionalize a visiting professor/lecture program. This will increase the number of underrepresented minorities in the classroom as well as exposing students and faculty to the untapped resources in our nation. Lectureships would range from a day or week, to a year. Every department on campus should participate.

- Establish collaborative and/or cooperative relationships with minority artists and other community organizations by featuring or sponsoring minority programs on campus. Not only will this expose majority audiences to diverse art, but will also emphasize the importance of diverse programming on campus.

BIBLIOGRAPHY

Abid-Nader, J. (1991, March). Strategies for motivating minority students. *Phi Delta Kappan,* 72, 546–549.

Anderson, J. A. (1991, January). The politics of retention: Rhetoric vs. reality. *Black Issues in Higher Education,* 7 (24), 116.

Auster, C. J. & McClelland, K. E. (1990, Nov/Dec). Public platitudes and hidden tensions: Racial climates at predominantly white liberal arts colleges. *Journal of Higher Education,* 62 (6), 607–642.

Bennett, C. (1991, March). Toward a multicultural curriculum. *American Association for Higher Education Black Caucus,* 1 (3), 1–4.

Blackwell, J. E. (1990, June). Operationalizing faculty diversity. *American Association Bulletin,* 8–9.

Canclatore, J. (1991, January). Recruitment and retention: What works. *Black Issues in Higher Education,* 7, 40–42.

Carter, D. & Chandler, A. (1991, April). Fostering a multicultural curriculum: Principles for presidents. *American Association of State Colleges and Universities,* 2–8.

Clay, C. A. (1990, Summer). Creating an affirming climate. *Metropolitan Universities: An International Forum,* 61 (2), 41–51.

Crews, A. C. (1990, December). Needed: Real agents for change. *Black Issues in Higher Education,* 7 (21), 72.

Duane, J., Parson, L. A. & Sands, R. G. (1991, Mar/Apr). Faculty mentoring faculty in a public university. *The Journal of Higher Education,* 62 (2), 176–193.

Finn, C. E., Jr. (1990, July). Point of view. *The Chronicle of Higher Education,* 36, A40.

Leo, J. (1990, November). A fringe history of the world. *U. S. News and World Report,* 109 (12), 25–26.

Levitz, R. & Noel, L. (1990, Summer). The retention challenge: It can be met. *Metropolitan Universities: An International Forum,* 1 (2), 31–39.

Milne, J. & Priest, D. (1991, Winter/Spring). A next step in student retention: Academic advising. *Journal for Higher Education Management,* 7, 36–37.

Shaw, K. (1991, Winter). Diversity on campus: Welcoming new members. *Educational Record,* 72, 6–13.

Wiley, E., III. (1990, December). How deep is the stated commitment to diversity? *Black Issues in Higher Education,* 7 (21), 1,6-7.

10

Queenie: A Case Study on Racial, Cultural and Gender Dimensions of Leadership

JOSEPHINE D. DAVIS

Within two months of her appointment as the new provost of Western State College (WSC), Dr. Jane Carson received notification that a legal suit was being filed against the institution. Mrs. Rosemary Benson, a part-time WSC student, filed the suit after losing her position as an elementary school teacher. She was terminated for failing a course required for renewing her teaching certificate.

According to Mrs. Benson, WSC professor Dr. John Watson terminated mid-semester the independent study course in which she had enrolled during the spring. Refusing to make provisions for Mrs. Benson to complete the course under a substitute instructor, Dr. Watson subsequently awarded her a failing grade at the end of the semester. By June, WSC officials notified Mrs. Benson that her appeal for a grade change had been denied. She immediately contacted a lawyer to file suit against the college.

The suit was presented during semester break at WSC. Few administrators were on campus. In the absence of the academic dean, the new provost asked the registrar to brief her on the Benson case. He substantiated the facts as reported by Mrs. Benson, then said resolutely, "Dr. Watson has a reputation for mistreating students. This isn't the first time a situation like this has occurred. If I were you, I'd do as your predecessors have done…refund the student's tuition and advise her to take the course at another institution."

Student enrollment was down at WSC, intensifying the likelihood of a significant midyear budget cut. In times like these, the provost realized that institutions needed to be more than accommodating to the academic and service interests of students. Yet, with no alternative course of action, Provost Carson reluctantly accepted the registrar's advice. However, she resolved to address this problem at a more substantive level.

When the education dean returned to campus in September, among the mail awaiting him was a letter from the new provost. She requested him to review with Dr. Watson the circumstances of the Benson case, then provide her a follow-up report. "If, indeed, you discern from your conference with Dr. Watson that the facts are verified as reported, have him to understand that such behavior will no longer be acceptable at WSC," Dr. Carson wrote.

Dr. Watson was so incensed by this conference with the dean that he could not contain himself. In lieu of waiting for the dean to present his concerns to the new provost, Dr. Watson wrote a letter which stated in part the following:

Dear Jane,

...let me get you straight on how we do business at Western State. You don't tell me how to run my classes. I'll cancel them when and if I want to. You better learn this fast if you intend to have a long tenure as provost at WSC...

Having arrived at WSC from a university where administrators were accorded utmost respect and adherence to academic protocol, and institutional policies were the norm, Dr. Carson was taken aback by the letter. First, the faculty member addressed an administrator on a first name basis. Secondly, he openly declared intentions to disregard institutional policies.

Two years earlier, WSC had hired its first African American administrator. Provost Carson was the second African American and second female administrator at the college. Since the Watson letter so disregarded and disrespected the authority of the Office of the Provost, the provost wondered whether Dr. Watson would have written a similar letter to her white male predecessors. She decided to discuss this perception with office colleagues. To a person, the letter was surprising. No one had ever seen or heard of another WSC administrator receiving such a "professionally and personally objectionable letter," each responded.

After a lengthy discussion with the affirmative action officer (AAO), Dr. Carson decided informal inquiries should be made of Dr. Watson's colleagues. The AAO was to discern the view of his unit. The AAO reported that the majority of Dr. Watson's colleagues and the secretaries "feared his wrath." He harassed women constantly. However, no one dared file formal complaints against him for fear of reprisal from his wife, who was his departmental chairperson. One secretary indicated that another faculty member had volunteered to complete the independent study course for Mrs. Benson. Dr. Watson refused the offer of help and was observed screaming at the student as she sought an explanation for his denial of her right to complete the course. The AAO said there were many other examples of Dr. Watson's repeated harassment of women.

Owing in part to the lack of collegial governance on campus (there was an entrenched we/they governance climate between the administration and the union), Dr. Watson refused Dr. Carson's request to meet and discuss the concerns of his letter to her. He instead sent the department's grievance officer and the president of the faculty union to confer with her on his behalf. Dr. Carson met for several hours with the union representatives. Ultimately, she was convinced by their arguments that Dr. Watson's intentions were questionable. A stalemate was reached using the protocol of collective bargaining.

Yet, Dr. Carson was not comfortable with the unresolved challenge to the authority to the Office of the

Provost, especially now that union officials were involved. "Would other faculty be encouraged to 'take on' the provost in WSC's hostile climate for campus governance? How could one achieve broad academic goals if faculty prerogatives were permitted to overrule institutional policies?" she wondered.

Dr. Carson then decided it was time to to engage the WSC president, Dr. Kline, in this dilemma. She wanted to apprise him of her interests to have the faculty clarify his intentions using, as a last resort, the only opportunity management has, the affirmative action process. President Kline agreed that something needed to be done. He dropped his head at the end of their conference and with a sigh said, "Do what you have to do."

The next day, President Kline sent his lawyer to advise Dr. Carson that he would not support her if she filed a formal affirmative action complaint against the faculty. "You're on your own," the attorney said.

Obtaining a second opinion from Attorney Richard Jackson, the Affirmative Action Officer for the University System, Dr. Carson was encouraged to advance a formal complaint against the faculty. Himself an African American and, as the AAO for the university system, experienced in the intricacies of campus politics on diversity, Attorney Jackson was adamant in advising Dr. Carson to take action, telling Dr. Watson, "You've got to file charges against this faculty member. We've got to show these people that African American administrators deserve to be treated with respect."

Dr. Carson returned to WSC and immediately filed a formal affirmative action complaint of gender harassment against Dr. Watson. A broad statement requesting his attention to improved relationships with women in his department was also placed in his personnel file.

The affirmative action complaint was not resolved at the Step One hearing on campus. It was referred to the system level for a Step Two hearing. Attorney Jackson was assigned to conduct the hearing on WSC's campus. Much to Dr. Carson's surprise, Attorney Jackson convened the hearing by declaring, "It would be embarrassing for the college if the rumor went forth that a male professor had sexually attacked a female administrator. In reviewing the files on this case, I find no evidence of sexual harassment. I doubt seriously if there are even grounds for racial harassment charges. Therefore, I am going to task Provost Carson and Dr. Watson to remain in the room while the rest of us leave. The two of them need to negotiate a compromise solution to this case."

Left alone, Dr. Carson and Dr. Watson saw and spoke to each other for the first time. From across the table, Dr. Watson opened the conversation, "Look Jane, this can be made easy. You need to know that I don't have to answer to you or anybody else on this campus."

Dr. Carson responded with a series of rhetorical questions. "From whom do you request vacation leave? To whom do you report your course schedule? What responsibility do you have to your dean? Do you understand the relationship you should have with him as your supervisor?"

He replied, "I supervise myself."

Dr. Carson acknowledged the hopelessness of further discussion with Dr. Watson. She asked everyone to return to resume the hearing. When they were seated, she announced, "We have reached a stalemate. Obviously, our perspectives on faculty governance are so different that a compromise is virtually impossible."

Jumping up from the table and flailing his arms wildly as he crossed the room, the union grievance officer screamed in Dr. Carson's face, "Who do you think you are? Do you think you are some sort of queen?"

Calmly wiping his saliva form her face, Dr. Carson replied, "Dr. Watson can speak as he chooses to whomever he chooses in any way that he chooses. I reserve the right to determine to whom I shall listen and to which tone I shall respond."

"Well," retorted the officer, "what do we have to do to get you to remove that letter from his personnel file?"

"The least he could do is apologize to me for writing such a personally and professionally insulting letter," said Dr. Carson.

Attorney Jackson issued a ruling on the case before leaving campus that day. Dr. Carson lost the case. Dr. Watson was not declared guilty of harassment in any form. Two days later, Dr. Carson received a carefully worded, two-page letter of apology from Dr. Watson. He promised to reflect more seriously in the future on the implications of his language and tone of communications to women and people of color. As stated to the grievance officer, Dr. Carson, upon receipt of the letter of apology, removed the letter of concern from Dr. Watson's personnel file. The next semester he took an unpaid leave of absence from WSC.

Nothing of the like impaired the ability of the provost to lead the college during the remainder of her tenure at Western State College.

DISCUSSION

This case study has been reviewed by national and regional audiences. As expected, most respondents focus their discussions on the racial and gender dimensions of this case, leaving unexamined the more substantive and central issue in *Queenie,* namely, interpreting and managing institutional culture.

The Core Issue

Queenie is a narrative describing the accommodation phase of the exchange process when the two very different cultures of native and stranger clash. As the new provost, Dr. Carson is the stranger who, seeing a wrong, endeavors to correct it. She is oblivious that this normal expectation for faculty to adhere to institutional policies, based on her previous experience in academe, is a major departure with the laissez-faire governance structure at WSC. Although she was hired with a faculty mandate to bring structure into the environment, it became obvious over time that WSC faculty protected their privileges of self-governance and reinforced this stance via the hostile governance climate.

As the new provost sought to alter the cultural tenets of the native land, Dr. Watson, now in the role of cultural bearer, issues her a warning. As the saga of *Queenie* unfolds, one observes the new provost, Dr. Carson, meeting with other colleagues in a search for meaning and interpretations of this new institutional culture. Unfortunately, her colleagues are not able to bridge for her the cultural gap. There are two reason for this. They were unfamiliar with the new provost's expectations based on the principles and tenets she understood of a very different institutional culture. Also, the WSC mentality is *win/win*. Listeners are indulged and basically reinforced in their expectation. Confrontations is avoided at all costs.

Having been reassured that her views were correct, Dr. Carson is left to interpret the subtle cultural symbols as bias-related behaviors. Reassured that her white male predecessors were never treated in this regard, Dr. Carson logically concludes that the differential treatment she receives must be explained by the remaining variables of gender and race.

Queenie also demonstrates how people of color cannot rely exclusively on members of their own race to serve as cultural guides in a foreign land. The guide's effectiveness may be compromised by issues of security. Recall, for example, the personal principles to assure an outcome in the case favorable to the system. Whether willingly or not, the token employee of color fulfills, quite effectively, the gatekeeping function. The *status quo* is maintained as pressures counter the propensity to balance individual principles with system goals.

Managing Institutional Culture

At some level, Provost Carson learned some of the tenets of the institutional culture at WSC on her own initiative—laissez-faire administration, a reactive versus proactive system, tribal warfare as a means of resolving issues, and informality. The difficulty Dr. Carson encountered in her efforts to manage the culture was the lack of support given by her supervisor, President Kline. In hindsight, he should have provided some assurances of how her predecessors managed the situation in a similar manner, as was done by the registrar. His advice was enabling. President Kline simply concluded, "I will not support your affirmative action complaint." What he would support to orient the new provost into the environment was not made clear. His actions, while consistent with the laissez-faire management style with which he governed WSC, did not serve the provost well.

Racial and Gender Issues

In national and regional discussion of this case study, white Americans express difficulty understanding why the provost was persistent in her pursuit of respect and dignity for herself and the Office of the Provost. White male respondents typically conclude, "Provost Carson needs to learn to choose her battles." For people of color, claiming respect and retaining personal dignity is a major battle. Most minorities are besieged with daily messages and actions which reflect the propensity of the dominant society to invalidate their heritage, worth and contribution. For them, self-esteem is enmeshed with the level of respect and dignity accorded.

Regarding the issue of gender differences, the role of language and communication tone feature prominently. Male administrators tend to be socialized to a a higher tolerance level of abusive language than most females. The typical female response to this case study is that gender harassment charges should have been filed against the grievance officer. Secondly, women take offense at Attorney Jackon's substitution of sexual harassment (with the implications of physical and explicitly sexual abuse) for gender harassment (where the implications were verbal and emotional abuse). This use of language is a ploy to discredit and undermine the real issues of the case.

The Lost Agenda

Queenie demonstrates how real agendas in the academy may often be lost to personal agendas. The real issue of institutional accountability to the student, Mrs. Benson, is lost. It is dismissed with the tuition refund and never addressed again. At WSC, the personal politics, the lack of collegial governance, and the unaddressed issues of gender and ethnic diversity overshadow student concerns.

More case studies of this nature are needed to raise awareness levels of the subtle ways in which cultural dissonance is manifest in the academy. As the role of language and tone, values, communication modalities, decision-making strategies, and other concerns are examined within the framework of institutional culture and its management, perhaps the halls of ivy will be more readily diversified.

11

Eight Principles for Promoting Diversity with Dignity

JOSEPHINE D. DAVIS

At the root of societal declines are foolish practices that represent violations of correct principles. How many economic disasters, intercultural conflicts, political revolutions, and civil wars could have been avoided had there been greater social commitment to correct principles?

Stephen Covey
Principle Centered Leadership

Conclusions

Coloring the Halls of Ivy examines the personal and professional experiences of senior- and mid-level administrators of color in public colleges and universities across this nation. Regardless of institutional type (i.e., liberal arts, comprehensive, etc.) or the geographic location of the college or university, minority administrators encounter at least five common barriers that can potentially derail them. These barriers, which have been examined in detail throughout this volume, are: miseducation, paradigm paralysis, noncommitted or marginally committed leadership, resilient institutional culture, and racism and gender bias. To facilitate further the process of "coloring the halls of ivy," two of the most subtle of these barriers are summarized below. Following subsequently are recommendations of the eight guiding principles for achieving equity and excellence within the ranks of senior- and mid-level administrators in the academy.

Miseducation

Institutions that achieve gains in diversity characteristically have shared values and goals. Faculty, staff, administrators and stakeholders from the broader community work collectively to achieve these mutually derived goals. Diversity is valued for the strengths it brings to decision-making and to the advancement of the institution.

Within the campus community, consensus is attained on the meaning of diversity. Its definition is made evident through the consistent allocation of fiscal and human resources. In this way, the campus community is not "miseducated" by the mismatch of actions occurring in the margins between the rhetoric of diversity and institutional practices.

Miseducation occurs, for example, when the recruitment and retention of American's ethnic minorities are balanced on a zero-sum scale with the recruitment of white women and internationals. Equity is thwarted during the hiring procedure through the maintenance of, at the most, a one-difference factor with the existing core faculty. Equilibrium is thus maintained. To the contrary, in well-informed and well-educated environments, such adaptive patterns are perceived as such and are not adopted as strategies of choice for diversifying the academy at the margins.

Miseducation about the value of diversity also results when an environment is created to heighten conflict and competition for limited and shrinking resources among the few minority groups on campus. Often funding sources for education programs and activities designed to enlighten the campus about all the "isms"—ethnocentrism, ableism, racism, sexism, etc., are centralized. Access to these resources is generally not clearly defined and the financial base is usually insufficient to address any one of the "isms" at a quality level. These divisive and counterproductive tactics must be recognized and managed as such.

It is recommended that miseducation about the value of diversity be addressed in policy terms using a more outcome-oriented format such as:

1. Scheduling campus-wide seminars and workshops with the goal of developing an operational definition for diversity which is appropriate to the mission and baseline conditions of the campus.

2. Supporting curriculum development designed to bring integrity to the general education curriculum by infusing non-Western and gender-balanced perspectives. Establishing credit-hour requirements that ensure all students are sufficiently exposed to multicultural, gender and minority studies.

3. Establishing reward systems that validate mentoring relationships with minority faculty, staff and students; providing credits toward tenure for faculty advisement and other supportive extra-curricular activities directed toward the retention of minority faculty, students and administrators.

Paradigm Paralysis

Issues of power and control are the primary reasons for paradigm paralysis. On most predominantly white and male-dominated campuses, the nonminority perspective is synonymous with the campus perspective. To alter such age-old and ingrained traditions is to challenge comfort zones. Privileged individuals are not generally accepting of new and different paradigms.

Time is the essential factor in addressing this challenge to diversity and to gender acceptance. This barrier can at best be moderated by sensitivity training conducted by knowledgeable and experienced professionals of the same race and sex of the aggrieved party. Also, those who work with such aggrieved individuals should be cognizant that, for them, diversity is a process achieved only after the successful progression through the classical stages of "Death" and "Transitioning," namely, the ultimate acceptance of change. Based on the experiences recounted throughout *Coloring the Halls of Ivy*, these are:

- denial and detachment,
- outrage,
- negotiation,
- despair, and
- recognition.

SUMMARY

The following institutional indicators serve to promote diversity and should be incorporated as goals in diversity training programs for campuses.

- The institution is headed by a chief executive officer (CEO) who demonstrates consistently a strong commitment to ethnic diversity initiatives. He or she supports decisions made by minority administrators.

- The institution is headed by a CEO who provides fiscal resources in support of the operational definition of diversity inasmuch as the practices for disbursing funds make clear to all parties the operational definition of diversity.

- Governance boards or campus governance bodies at the institution have approved policy statements regarding diversity.

- The environment for institutional governance is collegial.

- The institution has a corps of minority faculty and administrators who have been at the institution for at least five years or more.

- Academic departments at the institution have a corps of tenured faculty who are active and productive scholars.

- There are shared values at the institution, and its mission is embraced by faculty and administration.

- There is a common institutional vision.

The following personal attributes promote success among minority administrators on predominantly white campuses:

- The ability to identify the condition of paradigm paralysis.

- Familiarity with and tolerance for the stages of transitioning through which many change-resistant individuals must advance progressively, and at their own pace.

- Recognition that "nipping in the bud" is one useful strategy for managing most opposition to diversity.

- Maintenance of a sense of humor.

Recommendations

The following eight principles are proposed for achieving diversity with dignity in academic administration.

Leadership

1. Institutional climate toward diversity is mediated by the decisions and actions of the college or university president.

2. Decision-making is timely and empathetic. It maximizes factors conducive to achieving a pluralistic and humane-centered community.

Power

3. Institutional goals and expectations for diversity are

managed through adequate funding and systematic oversight of personnel recruitment, retention and reward systems, and attrition.

4. Decision-makers at all levels demonstrate a commitment to shared values and competence in motivating goal-oriented behavior throughout the academy. Collaborative and participatory decision-making models are used widely.

Timing

5. The community understands fully that achieving diversity is a process, not a product. Success is best achieved using a mission-centered approach, employing timely and viable strategies for reaching goals in short- and long-term states.

6. A balance between risk taking and patience is used to facilitate progression of change-resistant personnel and systems through the classical stages of death and transitioning.

Personal Behaviors

7. To be comfortable with discomfort is virtuous.

8. To withstand backlash once risks have been taken is meritorious.

12

Epilogue: A Visionary Leader in Challenging Times

DEBRA H. LU
JUDITH KILBORN

Debra H. Lu is a Professor of Accounting at St. Cloud State University. She received her Ph.D. in Accounting and Management of Information from the University of Minnesota. Dr. Lu has received a faculty achievement award, is active in university and community service, and has served as an officer for the local Coalition Against Racism and member of the Board of Directors of the United Way of St. Cloud.

Judith Kilborn is an Associate Professor of English at St. Cloud State University. Dr. Kilborn received her Ph.D. in English from Purdue University. She teaches business and technical writing, directs a writing center and has supervised tutors for the university-wide Advanced Placement Program for minority students. She has also served on several campus and community committees concerned with racism.

INTRODUCTION

We will never forget the day a representative from York College came to conduct an on-site interview of faculty and administrators concerning a finalist in their search for the new president of York College—our Vice President of Academic Affairs, Dr. Josephine D. Davis. Shortly thereafter, Dr. Davis was appointed President of York College, the City University of New York (CUNY) in Jamaica, New York. With this, she became the first African American woman to be president of a senior college in the CUNY system.

During her tenure at St. Cloud State University, Davis was known for her ability to nurture, support and mentor students, faculty and administrators. She faced and overcame sustained opposition while making substantial contributions to the university. The impact of her presence has been both immediate and long-term.

Calling upon the experience of Dr. Josephine D. Davis, this essay offers an inside-out perspective of a minority administrator at a predominantly white institution. We feel Dr. Davis' story quantifies and reaffirms the contributions minority administrators make to predominantly white institutions amidst struggle and turmoil. We also feel that her story provides a model for women interested in combining their family and professional lives successfully. Therefore, we have gathered information from a variety of sources, including eight administrators and faculty members, along with Dr. Davis herself, to relay as informatively and effectively as possible the challenges and success of one woman's significant and positive impact within an educational institution.

AN AFRICAN AMERICAN ADMINISTRATOR'S EXPERIENCE

Josephine Davis was raised in the segregated South and her recollections of this era are images molded by Jim Crow signs requiring colored to "sit from the rear" and drink from "Colored Only" water fountains. Dr. Davis was a product of the separate, and unequal, education system. As she recalls, the inside cover of her fourth-grade spelling book was stamped, "Discarded by the public schools of Virginia." Later in life, following her first year at Spelman College, she returned home to find a summer job. The employment representative offered her two: cooking and cleaning as a maid in white peoples' homes or performing very hard and strenuous manual labor in pulpwood, a position that only men held. The racist intent of these offers further encouraged Dr. Davis' desire to transcend society's imposed obstacles and barriers.

According to Davis, her strong belief in self and the promise that she could make a difference are attributed to the role models she had within her family. She was surrounded by people who were supportive and complementary to a pioneering spirit. First and foremost is her father, who encouraged Davis to travel and embrace a global view, telling her, "The world is yours to conquer." And 'conquer' is exactly what she did. At age eighteen, she went to Africa; at twenty-two she traveled throughout Eurasia and studied for a year in France at the Université de Besancon. Davis recalls a great aunt who was a minister in the 1930s, and traveled abroad throughout her career—a courageous endeavor considering the time. Davis' paternal grandmother, also a minister, traveled throughout the United States and modeled for Davis the life of a woman who managed to combine, successfully, family and career interests. Another strong female presence was her paternal aunt who was a high school principal in south Georgia during the 1940s and 1950s. Davis credits this aunt with convincing the Regents of the state of Georgia to make a policy exception, thus allowing Davis scholarship support to attend a private, rather than public, college. Overall, her family encouraged her interests in other cultures, provided a basis for the spiritualism which is a central part of her life, and supported her academic pursuits.

A world traveler, she has visited eleven African countries, traveled to all but three European countries, and visited Japan and China. As a scholar, she networks with education experts and conducts research with colleagues in Europe and Africa. Her research focus is racial and ethnic educational issues—teaching and learning in mathematics, and academic leadership development. Her experiences as a Kellogg Fellow enhanced her growth as a sensitive educator with a global perspective. As a Fellow, she spent a day with the homeless to understand their life circumstances better. She also visited slave castles, first in Nigeria and then later in Ghana and Senegal. About this, Davis states:

> I can't describe the intensity of the experience for you. Chains were draped around my neck, the actual chains used during the slavery era. The weight of those chains forced my body to the ground. Such inhumanity is difficult to describe. While I have seen slaves in chains in the movies, the reality of the weight and the emotional duress of being chained are incomprehensible. Prior to this time, I found it difficult to believe that the educational deficits of African American children were traceable to slavery. After this slave castle experience, I say forthrightly, yes. It is true. The emotional trauma of the slave experience was so overwhelming that it has transcended generations.

While Davis' Kellogg Fellowship and the broad network of friends and colleagues she met through it are indicative of the leadership qualities required of a visionary leader, she makes clear the importance of people-centered skills in effective leadership.

Davis' people-centered skills, i.e., interests in the welfare of other people and in the betterment of the community, are best illustrated through her understanding and sensitivity toward a Chinese graduate student. Within six months of her arrival at the university, the student went into a deep depression which affected her health and studies. She had made air reservations to return to China, but had mixed emotions about the trip home. According to Chinese tradition, for the student to return to China without a degree would be a failure in the eyes of everyone who loved her and had great expectations for her. Compounding the student's stress was the political climate in China. It was during the height of the Tiananmen Square uprisings. Aware of Chinese tradition and the strain it had to be causing the student, Davis approved sick leave for her and requested the designated college official to process the United States immigration form expeditiously so that her husband and young daughter could join her in the United States. An American sponsor had already been identified; the remaining challenge was to expedite the forms. Davis felt it was important to help this student achieve her career goals and return to an emotionally secure state of mind.

Dr. Davis' willingness to take that extra step to find solutions enables people to see beyond limitations, both personal and those imposed by others. Furthermore, her keen interests in people as individuals rather than as anonymous products of an institution assists her in promoting diversity throughout the campus and beyond.

As with her students, Davis appreciates, respects and empowers those who work with her. She reaffirms self-worth and ability, raises ambitions and professional goals, and follows-up by providing opportunities to act on these ambitions and achieve goals. According to Chief Academic Officer David Carr, Davis assisted him in reaching a greater understanding of his position as an academic leader. Upon learning of his interest in the integrated approach to higher education, Davis introduced Carr to the American Association of State Colleges and Universities Leadership Academy, accessing pertinent resources for him.

Reflecting on her view of leadership, Dr. Davis acknowledges that being a positive person and having the ability to understand people are essential:

> I'm a possibility thinker. I really believe in being a positive person and being goal-oriented. The essence of visionary leadership is understanding a wide-range of diverse people in different settings. It

is a demonstration of the ability to care for people and to facilitate their progression toward their mutually derived goals. I've seen people at their lowest, and I've seen them at their best. What I have concluded is that, if you genuinely care about people, if the people really want to better themselves, there's something within them that can be tapped. The ability to know people, to read people, to understand them is crucial to the success of the visionary leader.

Dr. Davis' vision, then, includes her wish to actualize possibility, to tap into people's desire to advance, and to empower that development

Mentoring

One of Dr. Davis' approaches to "empowering change" is through mentoring. The Assistant Vice President for Curriculum and New Programs, Linda Lamwers, tells of the guidance Davis provided her. Specifically, Davis encouraged Lamwers to apply for a fellowship from the American Association of State Colleges and Universities Leadership Program. Lamwers was assisted in defining her objectives and in rethinking her career plans to better support these established objectives. Davis' input resulted in Dr. Lamwer's strengthened position for upward mobility. In this instance, mentoring meant more to Dr. Davis than an offering of encouragement. Rather, it meant sharing valuable and practical experiences which had been well-tested.

Davis compassionately mentored faculty as well. In one instance, Davis mentored Associate Professor of Applied Psychology Zoa Rockenstein. Davis enabled her to move into an administrative position as the Director of the

Honors Program. Davis introduced Rockenstein to various university constituencies so that she would be familiar with influential names and faces, and have a good start when she assumed her new administrative responsibilities.

Davis is exceptionally supportive and active in the mentoring of faculty of color. Tamrat Tademe, an Ethiopian faculty member and Assistant Professor in the Department of Human Relations and Multicultural Education, describes how Davis went beyond the call of duty in furthering his standing at the university:

> She has made my talents visible. I am a political scientist, but my expertise is in Africa, Afro-Centricity, and African Americans in the United States as well as in Africa. She supported a research project that I did with Dr. Bassey Eyo on Afro-Centricity. She helped us on research and provided us support, more than material assistance. She organized workshops on our behalf to make our knowledge available to the rest of the campus community.

Dr. Davis' recognition of Tademe's talent and provision of opportunities for him to demonstrate his talent to colleagues sent a message. According to Tademe, her actions said, "This person is capable and has something to contribute." Tademe notes that this approach provides minority faculty with credibility, which is crucial to forward movement. Tademe also points out Davis' habit of continuously validating the contributions of minority faculty in the eyes of their colleagues. He indicates that without recognition by a person in power, it is extremely difficult for faculty of color to be effective.

Davis' validation of the worth of faculty of color is important for their retention. However, such empowerment is universal, rather than limited to faculty of color, and is a hallmark of Davis' leadership style. This aspect includes her ability to work with people, her global and integrated vision of higher education, her strong sense of fairness and justice, and her insights on conflict resolution.

Team- and Consensus-Building

Davis' ability to motivate faculty and administrators to work effectively as members of a team is a skill central to her successful leadership. Davis continuously reminds her colleagues that they are not by themselves, they are a part of a team. She makes it known to individuals that they are not fighting an uphill battle alone—others are available to assist and guide if need be. According to Lamwers, this promotes people's active participation in building a consensus:

> She is very visionary. She tries to bring people in. She tries to make decisions and look forward with input from other people. She isn't out there by herself, with the troops four thousand miles behind. One of her strengths is her ability to bring other people to consensus....She makes the decision, but she asks for all sorts of input, consensus, and uses the team-building approach in doing that.

For Davis, the key aspects of team-building are delegation of responsibility and the sharing of power. According to Rockenstein, "She has a strong belief that the more power you have, the more power you have to give away. This is one of the first things she told me: 'Being in a high place was not a position of controlling other people but of delegating power.'"

Davis encourages a participatory form of problem-solving meant to build consensus as well as to tie decisions to a more global vision. In promoting such a process,

Davis fosters transformation of the institution. In fact, Carr sees her leadership as *transformational.* Referring to what is called a transformational leader, Carr explains how Davis tries to take institutions to new levels, to establish a vision and work toward its fruition. As a transformational leader, part of working towards a vision and engaging people in problem-solving is conflict resolution. The more people involved in achieving institutional goals, the more complicated the nature of the task. This results in more conflicts within the institution. "Therefore," Davis comments, "conflict resolution is, in a sense, all I do."

Dr. Davis' ability to resolve conflict is based upon her ability to distinguish between the superfluous and the true issue or issues underlying conflict. Carr explains Davis' problem-solving strengths:

> She is good in decision-making. I would say her skill is in tying decisions back to a central integrating principle by asking herself and others: What are we doing here? What is our purpose? What is right? What is our vision? Where are we trying to go? By doing this, decisions aren't what I call 'idiosyncratic' and isolated from what's happening. Rather, decisions are tied to larger purposes.

Davis realizes that if conflicts are to be resolved, the root of the problem must be discovered; otherwise, the conflict will return in another form. In Davis' words, "Usually what you're dealing with in the conflict is not its essence. First you experience the cloud, then the smoke. Finally, after great deliberation, you arrive at the essence of the problem....You never resolve the conflict without addressing the core of the problem."

In conflict avoidance situations people often give politically correct reasons for their actions. For example, hiring women faculty is a laudable thing; however, it can also be a rationalization for not hiring a person of color. Davis said, "I offered this cultural diversity position to the department. The first question the department asked me was, 'Can we hire a white woman with expertise in the field of diversity?' Often such questions are smoke screens." What Davis inferred from the department's question was that they did not accept the challenge to hire racial and ethnic minorities as central to promoting the cultural diversity agenda. "Hiring a white woman was not the issue here; this faculty didn't want to hire someone drastically different from what they were accustomed," said Davis.

Davis understood that the fear of differences fueled the department's reaction to the challenge. Clearly, problem-solving is dependent upon how well one understands his or her environment. In this case, a class action suit had increased the percentage of women faculty and administrators at the university. Thus, to this department, hiring women was a politically correct way of rationalizing. Obviously, they had not yet come to truly understand the need for cultural diversity.

Davis knows that understanding the environment and culture of a department or institution is essential in uncovering people's motives, emotions and fears. Without such understanding, problem-solving is near impossible. According to American Indian and Director of Human Relations and Multicultural Education flo wiger, Davis is very adept at analyzing problems and encouraging creative solutions within specific contexts:

> I see her as someone who is able to come in, look at situations, identify problem areas...and develop creative solutions. They are not solutions that are top-down. They are solutions in which she involves people, brings in people and says, 'Here is

the problem. What do you think needs to be done, and how can I help you to do it?'

Davis searches behind the smoke to get to the root of the problem. She is willing to set issues on the table and to encourage cooperative resolution of them.

RESISTANCE

In many higher education institutions, people who are different from the majority are not always welcomed wholeheartedly. As an African American woman in a high ranking administrative position, Davis encountered racism and sexism during her stay at the university. The campus did not have any experience with working with leaders of color. Tademe points out:

> Generally, this campus is not used to people of color. If it's used to people of color, it's used to people of color who are quiet. They want us to have the color but not the culture. If you are a person who has a leader's vision, who is not a follower, and if you are a person of color, you are resisted. Davis was resisted.

This resistance is, of course, not only because of her race, but also because she is a capable female. Davis states:

> The struggle for me has just come lately. It's been a struggle of recognition as a woman, a capable woman. Even in my previous institution, where I was a black person in a black institution, some men felt threatened by my competence. My supervisor was a male and had difficulties interacting with me. It's not just race always; it's also a feminist issue…it is also a question of dignity.

Davis received inadequate institutional support and a lack of commitment as shown through racist and sexist acts. When Davis was hired as Vice President for Academic Affairs, her appointment was a symbolic gesture to fulfill a cultural diversity mandate. However, inadequate support prevented her from realizing fully the goals she set out to accomplish. Additionally, because of her color, Davis was not accorded the respect and courteous treatment normally conferred upon people in positions of authority. Tademe describes how this phenomenon generally manifests itself for administrators of color:

> When you are an administrator of color, the protocols that employees, the people who work under you, and the white administration follow, are ignored. They don't provide you the respect they usually give to their white colleagues.

In Davis' case, instead of being mentored into the system, empowering her, most often she was cut out of the loop. Indications of ignored protocol could be as subtle as the way in which fellow administrators seated themselves at a meeting. flo wiger said:

> I watched how members of the administration would all take their places and would sit at specific places, often taking the head seat before Davis entered the room....It was interesting for me to watch this because I thought, if she were a male, if she were not black, they would not have done this—*she* would be the one logically to sit at the head of the table.

Another clear case of personalized racism was demonstrated when three administrators—Davis, a black male, and Lamwers, who is a white female—were invited to present a panel discussion on collective bargaining and assessment at a national conference. After they returned, the white female discovered that, even though there were no university faculty present during the panel, a faculty member was planning to file a grievance against Davis and the black male administrator for talking about the university during a national presentation. In describing this situation, Lamwers pointed out that she, the only white administrator, was not mentioned as part of the grievance. During a lengthy conversation, Lamwers had to explain to a faculty association representative that neither Davis, nor the black male administrator, had spoken about the university at all:

> I have a copy of my presentation, and if you want to have it, you can have it. Josephine [Davis] just gave her own view of the accreditation process and collective bargaining in general. The other presenter gave some specific examples of how you might resolve some of the issues involved. If there is anybody who said anything about the institution, it was me.

The lack of trust apparent in this example, with its clear roots in racist attitudes, was typical during Davis' tenure at the university. Davis was situated in the midst of a campus unaccustomed to leaders of color. She was surrounded by opposition, lack of commitment to her success as a leader, inadequate support and respect, racist behavior and sexual harassment. As time went on, it became obvious that the institution was not prepared to accept diversity as fact, but only as rhetoric.

Davis' approach to dealing with the continuous bombardment of racist attacks is to continually reaffirm her vision of herself, stay in contact with the strong support group of Kellogg Fellows, and keep a positive attitude about life. She states:

> Creative visualization is the answer. Then one must do whatever is necessary to make the vision possible. There is a need to hold onto the vision, although numerous distractions may occur. Be careful not to internalize or own all things negative....I believe in nurturing myself in positive ways. If I must endure distractions and people who know a thousand and one reasons why something will not work, I give them an audience, but I do not absorb their negativism.

AFFECTING CHANGE IN A HOSTILE ENVIRONMENT

Despite the turmoil and opposition Davis experienced at the institution, she accomplished much. Certainly, many of her contributions were in the area of cultural diversity initiatives. However, the changes Davis made were broader in scope; for they also included integrating and streamlining academic affairs' operations and procedures, globalizing the curriculum, improving the quality of undergraduate, graduate, and international studies programs, and obtaining significant external funding for the institution.

Davis began the transformation of the university from an institution that professed cultural diversity to an institution that practiced cultural diversity. She insisted on the importance of truly understanding and making a real commitment to implementing cultural diversity. This has meant changing the ways in which administrative and faculty searches were conducted, newly hired minority faculty were mentored, minority students were advised, and resources were distributed.

She has been instrumental in developing and obtaining external funding for the Advanced Preparation Program (APP) for minority students, a program in which minority students complete eight credits of math and English the summer after their high school graduation. The APP and the mentoring program which matches each minority student with both a faculty advisor and a student mentor, usually an upper class student of color, have increased minority student retention considerably. Davis is also responsible for the development of a videotape for faculty orientation to help faculty become more sensitive to minority students' needs. In addition, Davis suggested that the writing center director develop a multicultural collection of student writing and artwork to help promote minority student use of center services as well as provide minority students with a vehicle for their creativity. Given Davis' encouragement and financial support, this literary collection, titled *Kaleidoscope,* is now moving into annual publication.

Cultural diversity initiatives regarding American Indians emerged under Davis' support. Davis initiated work on a proposal for an American Indian Studies minor. According to American Indian and Associate Professor of English Steve Crow, who worked on the proposal, the project would never have started without Davis. Both Crow and wiger credit Davis with establishing a relationship for the first time with the Mille Lacs Band of Chippewa Indians. According to wiger, Davis sought and was granted funds for Mille Lacs teachers to attend a summer training program and for the university's faculty to go to Mille Lacs and work with the teachers from the reservation. With Davis' support, new possibilities for communication between American Indians and the university were made possible.

Davis reorganized the academic unit, consistent with some longstanding recommendations that had been made by several accreditation review teams. She also insisted upon accountability for resources and encouraged the development of annual reports. She was instrumental in preparing policy manuals which contained all the policies for academic affairs in one central source. She was responsible for developing one document containing information concerning aspects of the university such as its total square footage and its total computing capabilities to aid in the writing of grant proposals. She was also responsible for getting a three-day period for fall faculty orientation, allowing faculty more time to explore the issues of higher education before rushing into classes. Moreover, she has, according to Lamwers, "really worked hard to make the deans a team. There is much greater respect among the deans for one another and much more collegial interaction. Before they operated more independently and much more competitively with one another." Davis also was instrumental in improving the working relationship between the faculty association and the administration. flo wiger comments that Davis worked very hard to move the faculty association and the administration toward a cooperative and a collaborative model.

Davis' emphasis on the quality of educational programs has encouraged action in many areas. Her emphasis on formalized institutional goals and objectives has facilitated the development of both college and departmental goals and objectives. She orchestrated the North Central Association accreditation team visit to ensure its success. In addition, Davis' effort to transform graduate education into an institution-wide priority has begun to move the institution into a truly comprehensive university.

Davis gave the institution a more global vision and an internationalized curriculum. One colleague says that Davis, with her extensive travel experience, "looks at the world with a global perspective as opposed to a local perspective." Her internalization of the curriculum includes Multicultural, Gender, and Minority (MGM) courses required for general education so that graduates are prepared with a more global vision as they move into the workplace. Encouraging faculty participation in curriculum development was also significant. In the area of international studies programs, Davis visited all of the international studies sites and encouraged the faculty to make their coursework abroad more relevant and more germane to current issues. Contributing substantially to program development as well is Davis' active involvement in grant writing which generated over 1.5 million dollars in one academic year.

Conclusion

Throughout her tenure as Vice President for Academic Affairs, Josephine Davis injected the transformational perspective into the academic environment, and a substantial part of her legacy is empowerment. This institution is now more capable and more willing to shape its own future. She understood that she alone couldn't perform the giant task of educating our youth, and that we need many more leaders in education. When she identifies people with leadership qualities, Davis extends herself, unselfishly mentoring people, investing in them, and opening doors for them. Summarizing Davis' two years at the university, the Director and Assistant Vice President for Research said, "The full impact of what she has set in motion won't be felt for about five years to come. Her style is to challenge. Her long-term impact to this institution is the infusion of new ideas and perspectives into everything we do."

Dr. Davis has empowered many of us through her mentoring and support. We believe that she will have a significant impact on higher education nationally. As Rockenstein so aptly said, "Josephine Davis is going to be a great shining light in higher education, in a way that will transcend race, gender, and historical patterns."

Recommendations

Dr. Davis' experiences at St. Cloud State University can be generalized to provide guidelines for: 1) administrators of color who wish to work at predominantly white campuses, and 2) universities that would like to hire and retain minority administrators.

To Administrators of Color. Administrators of color who would like to gain employment at predominantly white campuses should prepare themselves for the environment they will encounter. They must hone their communication and interpersonal skills and develop a tough skin so that they can deal with racist behavior, personal harassment and indignities. They must become risk-takers who are unafraid of personal attacks. They should seek out opportunities for individual growth, travel and development of interests in other cultures to enhance their global vision.

When searching for jobs and interviewing, administrators of color should research schools thoroughly, talking with minority administrators, faculty, staff, and students on campus to gain insights into both the positive and negative experiences of minority people. In particular, they should identify whether the institution provides a positive environment for personal growth as well as opportunities to contribute to the institution.

Once minority administrators have accepted positions, they should study the environment carefully, network to gain support on campus, build coalitions in solving problems and mediating conflict, and serve as agents of change.

It is important to understand not only university policies and procedures, but also the history of the institution and the way things are traditionally done. To be successful, administrators of color should appreciate and empower those who work for them. Generously sharing credit with people is one way to gain long lasting support. Administrators of color can also gain support on campus by serving as mentors and role models for others. In addition, they can gain support by being sensitive to faculty, staff and students' needs and by providing assistance.

Many administrators of color will discover that their mere presence on predominantly white campuses will affect change. By tapping into people's desire to change, they can facilitate that change. Nevertheless, it is essential that minority administrators understand their environment and realize that change is difficult and painful. When conflicts arise and problems must be solved, support can be garnered if administrators of color develop consensus through the delegation of responsibilities and the sharing of power. Experience ensures this course of action promotes and sustains an environment conducive to forward movement and a spirit of collegiality.

To Universities that Wish to Retain Administrators of Color. If universities wish to hire and retain administrators of color, campus leaders must demonstrate a serious and sincere commitment to cultural diversity. They must make it clear that affirmative action does not end with the act of hiring. In particular, the president should make his or her support of the minority administrator apparent. This support includes acknowledgment of the administrator of color's contributions to the university and community. The university administration should also actively mentor administrators of color, familiarizing them with the local policies, procedures and history.

Most importantly, administrators, and the president in particular, should respond immediately to negative or incorrect comments made in public about or to an administrator of color. In summary, universities should establish both short- and long-term cultural diversity goals; specifically, they should address and acknowledge racist behavior and policies quickly, publicly and on an ongoing basis.

March 10, 1994

To Lea,
Best Wishes,
Josephine D. Davis